Voices From The Blue States

Voices From The Blue States

✦

Commentary From The Rest of America

Edited by Mack Williams

iUniverse, Inc.
New York Lincoln Shanghai

Voices From The Blue States
Commentary From The Rest of America

iUniverse books may be ordered through booksellers or by contacting:

iUniverse
2021 Pine Lake Road, Suite 100
Lincoln, NE 68512
www.iuniverse.com
1-800-Authors (1-800-288-4677)

ISBN-13: 978-0-595-36971-3 (pbk)
ISBN-13: 978-0-595-81377-3 (ebk)
ISBN-10: 0-595-36971-5 (pbk)
ISBN-10: 0-595-81377-1 (ebk)

Printed in the United States of America

Contents

The Nation

The War

Introduction

✦

"Reverse the Curse"

Once the Boston Red Sox failed to pull off their prospective 2003 winter trade for Alex Rodriguez—who was promptly snapped up by their hated and star-studded rival New York Yankees—most baseball fans would not have given the Sox a snowball's chance in Baghdad to win the 2004 World Series. Not only had Red Sox management lost the opportunity to acquire one of baseball's finest all-around players, they had to have engendered some big-time hurt feelings on the home front, as their star players Manny Ramirez and Nomar Garciaparra were slated to be traded to make the A-Rod deal work. Who could have predicted that the disgruntled Garciaparra would get sent to the similarly long-suffering Cubs, and Ramirez would wind up as the World Series most valuable player?

With all the jubilation in Red Sox Nation over their first World Series victory in 86 years, one could almost forget that the Red Sox have generally had very good teams on a consistent basis. Much of the joy Red Sox fans are experiencing is due to the disappointment they have felt so many times when top-notch Boston teams failed to get the job done in the clutch. As such, no feelings of surprise anyone may have over the Red Sox victory can compare with the shock felt in 1969 when the New York Mets…winners of only 40 out of 160 games in their inaugural 1962 season and not all that many more in any of the next six…defeated the great Baltimore Oriole team four games to one to become the most highly unlikely World Series champion in history.

Shortly after their improbable victory, the Mets' future Hall-of-Famer, ace pitcher Tom Seaver, stated that if the Mets could win the World Series, then perhaps the United States could get out of Vietnam. Adapting that sentiment for the twenty-first century, one might say that if the Red Sox can win their first World Series in 86 years, then perhaps the United States can get out of Iraq. Perhaps we can regain the respect we had from our allies and the community of nations. Perhaps we will come to the realization that questioning administration policy is not un-American, but in fact indicative of a great love of one's country—which brings us to this book.

"Voices From The Blue States" is a somewhat figurative title, especially since there are contributors that come from "red" states, as well as from the continent of Africa. That said, this book seeks to give voice to some of the 59 million people—and more, including those who did not register their opinions at the polls—that were greatly displeased with the results last November, that love this country and are horrified at the direction in which we are heading on several fronts.

The essays within this book range from long and analytical, to short and profound. Some proffered various solutions, while others came with commentary relative to our place in the world at present. In general, I asked contributors to simply share how they were feeling—and one, Sybil Baffoe of northern California, needed far less than a page to detail where she was.

"I was utterly disappointed with the voters from the red states. My mood has changed now, though. I've come to terms with the election results as I believe George MUST finish what he started and take full responsibility for the outcome of his actions beyond the first 4 years. This second term is his opportunity to prove himself since he does not have to win another election. Will he be motivated to leave a positive global legacy after 8 years in office? I'm holding out hope!"

Sybil cut right to the chase, in that sitting around having pity parties fails to advance our cause. Despite our disappointment, dissatisfaction and indeed, disgust, we must move forward and not only hope for the best, but work to insure that our desired outcomes will ultimately emerge. It is my hope that "Voices From The Blue States" will, at the very least, serve as a catalyst for discussion to this end.

Mack Williams
August, 2005

Preface

Editor's Note: The following piece, which I wrote during the buildup to the Iraq war, defined the actions of the President while he prepared for the conflict that he felt would define his presidency. Some two-plus years later, it serves as a backdrop for what is to come within these pages.

War & The Ten Commandments
March, 2003

If you were to spend a Sunday morning walking or riding through your neighborhood or community, you would find a considerable number of people who have no intention whatsoever of going to church. While each of these people would have his or her individual take on why they don't feel the need for a weekly dose of the Good News, one might find that a recurring theme among this group of people would be that of a lack of consistency in the messages that are being put forth by those in the church.

In other words, your talk don't match your walk. To that end, one need look no further than 1600 Pennsylvania Avenue, Washington, D.C. to find the world's preeminent example of this type of inconsistency, George W. Bush.

President Bush loves to talk about his faith, loves to be photographed with conservative African-American ministers, and so on and so on. However, his unabashed zeal for war with Iraq shows at best a lack of understanding of the religious tradition he professes belief in, and at worst, a total dissing of its' principles. A study of some of the Ten Commandments illustrates this.

"Thou shall not kill."
As we see the daily news broadcasts highlighting the technological advances made available to the armed forces in the years since the Gulf War, we can do nothing but assume that a war will kill thousands upon thousands of Iraqi citizens. Why is this death and destruction necessary, in light of the fact that Iraq has been restrained and contained for the twelve years since 1991?

"Thou shall not covet…anything that belongs to your neighbor."
The President and members of the administration speak of freeing the Iraqi people from Saddam Hussein but, ironically enough, some of these very same individuals were silent and exhibited no desire to free oppressed people when South African Blacks were living under the horrific apartheid regime of the Afrikaners.

They weren't so gung-ho about folks' freedom then, so what's the deal now? Many feel that the real reason the former oilman Bush wants to lead "a coalition" into Iraq—and by the way, the last time I checked in the dictionary, coalition did not mean "two"—is to gain access to Iraq's oil…which leads us to *"You shall have no other gods before me."* This administration is so intent on getting to this oil they so crave that they are eager to throw caution to the wind and American and Iraqi lives to the grave.

"You shall not give false testimony against your neighbor."
It seems, according to most of the world's nations, that the inspections are working—and are clearly deserving of more time. But President Bush tries his hardest to reinvent each universally acclaimed positive development as a sign that Iraq has not disarmed, and more reason to begin war sooner than later. He continues to imply that there are links between Iraq and Al-Qaeda, which all reasonable evidence does not support. And we all know that if Hans Blix and the inspection team found nothing more than David's slingshot, Bush would term that a "weapon of mass destruction" and would call for war. Once again, *"Thou shall not covet…anything that belongs to your neighbor."*

"Honor your father and your mother."
George W. Bush's mother, former first lady Barbara Bush, lost a child and saw her hair turn gray as a result of the shock, sadness and loss she understandably felt. Shouldn't the President be able to look at his own mother, envision the horror so many other mothers will feel as a result of a war, and attempt to avoid war at all costs?

My mother told me, at a very young age, that I should never start a fight—but if someone were to hit me, I should hit them once in retaliation for what they did, and once more to insure that they will refrain from doing that again. I have tried to follow that principle…but President Bush is of a different mindset. He wants to initiate this conflict just because he can, in spite of the views of much of his own nation and most of the rest of the world. What a dangerous concept, that of annihilating a nation just because you say that somewhere down the line they may want to attack you.

That is wrong. That is un-American. And that is why many people believe we need a "regime change" at 1600 Pennsylvania Avenue on November 2nd, 2004.

The Vote

An Open Letter from the Blue States

by Rev. W. Golden Carmon, Sr.

June, 2005

One of the most cherished documents of our nation proclaims, "We hold these truths to be self-evident, that all men [persons] are created *equal*, that they are endowed by their Creator with certain unalienable Rights that among these are Life, Liberty and the pursuit of Happiness." Equality, that unassailable principle which leads each of us, as American Citizens, to believe what Webster defines as having the same value, privileges, status, or rights. This principle resonated so strongly with our fore-parents, irrespective of their race, color or creed, that it gave them the resolve to change the course of history.

Many of us American Citizens, who live in the Blue States, are greatly concerned that the innate power of this principle is fast losing its prowess, in practice, in our times. Consider for example the plight of the elderly and families with inadequate or no access to affordable health care in the wealthiest nation on earth. It is unacceptable for 43 million Americans under the age of 65 to have no healthcare insurance and for the infant mortality rate for black Americans to be double that of white Americans, and four times that of Japanese. This is tragic when one realizes that healthcare accounts for nearly 14% of our country's gross domestic product, versus 8% for Japan and Britain (The Economist, October 2004). We ask the citizens of the Red States and the current administration: is the absence of affordable health care for all really equality?

We are also strongly concerned about the loss of millions of good paying jobs in our nation since 2000. No longer can politically motivated policy makers and misguided hate groups erroneously attribute this to the advances of the Civil Rights Movement or "Quotas," since few people of color had the latest round of

3

high wage, often high tech jobs that were lost. Nor can they be simply attributed to a bad economy or even that these jobs went to other nations. If this were so, the conventional wisdom of the incumbent national leadership would have us believe that their many rounds of tax cuts, which unquestionably disproportionately benefited high income earners and large businesses, should have slowed these prime job losses by now. We are expressly concerned that these prime job losses are attributed directly to the flawed economic policies and the highly questionable decision to go to war in Iraq. And we can only conclude that it appears the current administration chose the path of least resistance and self-interest—under the disguise or national interest. This appears especially true for the war since in their uninformed religious fervor, they seemed to be unaware that the Apostle Paul reminds us that vengeance belongs solely to God (Romans 12:16-21). We ask the citizens of the Red States and this current administration: is the loss of good paying jobs really equality?

We are further strongly concerned about the yet vast gap between educational initiatives and the corresponding necessary funding. We all know educators, already distracted from their primary mission of teaching, are now being asked to implement yet another national program ("No Child Left Behind" has become "Every Child Left Behind") with apparently very limited national funding. We must conclude that it is simply a program of political convenience at the expense of our dedicated teachers and all our precious children. Furthermore, considering the importance of college education to the long term economic viability of our nation (producing over 60% of the Nobel Prizes since World War II), and with the cost of a college education testing the limits of middle-class American resources, the disparity between the haves and haves-not has accelerated. We ask the citizens of the Red States and this current administration: is a quality education (K-12 and college) only for high-income Americans? Is cutting proven programs that give children from low-income families a head start in life really equality?

Each November through 2008 all eligible voters in the Red and the Blue States across America have an opportunity, an obligation, and a moral imperative to restore the legacy of equality our fore-parents died to pass on to us. This revolution however will not be won with muskets, but with voting ballots. How should you vote? We, the American Citizens of the Blue States strongly believe and urge you to prayerfully vote according to your conscience.

Since our votes each November change the course of history, like our fore-parents, we are compelled to put aside our personal interests, and let our conscience be guided by the words of the Prophet Jeremiah (22:1-3) in proclaiming God's mind to the political leaders of his day. "Act with justice and righteousness, and deliver from the hand of the oppressor anyone who has been robbed. And do not do wrong or violence to the stranger, the orphan, and the widow, nor shed innocent blood in this world." Only by voting for the local, state, and national candidates who meet this divine standard can *we the people* truly have "One Nation under God, Indivisible, with Liberty and Justice *for All.*"

Rev. W. Golden Carmon, Sr. is the pastor of the Mt. Zion AME Church in Plainfield, New Jersey.

A Vote Is a Terrible Thing to Waste

by Mack Williams

I found myself in agreement with a staunch Republican—who happens to be an African-American—during our recent discussion of the 2004 presidential election. He described it as one where the incumbent was saddled, on the international front, with what had become his unpopular war, while at home the previously robust economy was in a shambles. By all rights, such an incumbent should have never won.

Naturally George W. Bush capitalized on the post-September 11th fears of the nation, and rode those fears on to victory. Nonetheless, we are left to ask what the Democratic Party must do to return to prominence—to win—at the national level. This topic has been discussed from sea to shining sea since President Bush's re-election…which is actually a term one ought hesitate to use because of the implication that he had really won in the year 2000. That said, I would submit that revisiting the 2000 debacle—and the disenfranchisement of many thousands of Black folks in Florida—can show that part of the answer is right before our eyes.

We all know that Democrats need to reach out to various and different segments of the electorate—especially those that for one reason or another have bought into the rhetoric of the other party, even as that party's policies work against their true economic interests. It seems, however, that we have gotten so wrapped up in the pursuit of the so-called "Reagan Democrats"/"soccer moms"/ "NASCAR dads," and so on, that we have lost sight of the fact that African-Americans are the most consistent supporters that the Democratic Party has. Certainly the opposition has not forgotten, as evidenced by their documented efforts and various statements regarding suppression of the African-American vote. They know that in many cases if enough African-Americans vote, there is little chance that the Democratic candidate would lose.

If, for instance, I managed a major league baseball team and one of my players were batting .450, I can guarantee you he would not be on the bench. If LeBron James, Reggie Miller, Dwyane Wade or Diana Taurasi were on my basketball team, I would certainly see to it that they got and shot the ball.

One player does not a team make, nor does one segment of the population provide the sole key to electoral victory. But just as a coach would hope to get maximum production from his or her best player, shouldn't the Democratic Party do everything in its' power to garner the most possible votes from its' most reliable constituency, the African-American community? If you know that ninety percent of a particular group of people is going to support you, wouldn't it seem to be in your best interest to get as many of these people to the polls?

Of course, part of the problem may be that some in the Democratic establishment may not think outreach to the African-American community is needed. Ever since the campaign of 1960, when John F. Kennedy placed the phone call to Coretta Scott King while Dr. Martin Luther King was jailed, we have worked under the assumption that the Black vote would be overwhelmingly Democratic.

Meanwhile. the Republicans have given us little reason to think otherwise, since they have theorized—and, in fact, proven—that they can win without Black support, and have strategized accordingly. At the 2004 Republican convention, California Gov. Arnold Schwarzenegger's speech touched on how America rejoiced when South Africa's apartheid era ended. Much of America did indeed rejoice, and Mr. Schwarzenegger may have rejoiced with his in-laws, but quite a few of the people seated right in front of the Governor there in Madison Square Garden had not been supportive of the cause. That group might seem to include Vice-President Dick Cheney, who while serving in Congress voted several times against resolutions calling for the release of Nelson Mandela.

The mere fact, however, that Democrats provide a more palatable alternative to Republican policies does not necessarily mean that every African-American is going to rush to the polls. Some may need convincing that voting is the answer to our problems, or at least an important part thereof. Others may feel that the differences between the parties are barely more than marginal, or cosmetic in nature.

In each of these instances, I believe that a little of the same type of effort—and money—thrown at the soccer mom/NASCAR dad types would go a long way and ultimately yield tangible results. Those in the establishment, on the other hand, who try to minimize any visible association between the party and African-American concerns—so as not to "offend," if you will, any other valued segment of the electorate—are finding their efforts less productive.

The last example warrants further examination—because if the perception is that there is hardly any appreciable difference between the two parties, then the Democratic Party has failed, especially in light of the fact that polls consistently show that voters are more in agreement with traditional Democratic viewpoints. Naturally the fact that Iowa and New Hampshire—two of the least multi-cultural states in the union—are grandfathered into the front end of the presidential primary season doesn't seem to help, as the two provide a slim opportunity for a progressive candidate to emerge in the lead.

But beyond that, the factions in the party seeking to reposition Democrats into the center of the political landscape have led some people to view Democrats as almost being "Republican Lite." If this is the intent, the strategy is flawed, in that most people who prefer Republican policies would more than likely choose the butter over the margarine, the original over the likeness. While proponents of such a strategy like to point to President Clinton as their prime example of success, they fail to take into account the fact that Clinton is not just a mere centrist politician but a masterful communicator who has bonded with African-Americans and other voters of color in a way few politicians have in recent memory.

One of the classic poems that came out of the Harlem Renaissance era was Langston Hughes' "Let America Be America Again," in which Hughes longs for the day when America lives up to its' promise. As we move towards 2006, 2008, and beyond, we can only hope that Democrats will be Democrats again, and present themselves as clear alternatives to those whose policies make the world less safe and our nation less free.

A Voice from the Wilderness

by Susan Puder

Where can one start when talking about the last presidential election? Were we robbed like the 2000 election? John Kerry says he accepts the results from Ohio, but most of his supporters don't. But, does it make a difference that the GOP Secretary of State in Ohio ensured a win for Bush by providing fewer voting machines in the urban areas, where people lined up for hours to vote, some into the wee hours of the morning; and more in the affluent sections, where there was almost no wait? Or, how about the idea of not registering people using a form not on a certain weight paper? The Republican operatives under the direction of Boss Rove would make sure that Bush won again no matter what.

I was the Kerry coordinator for a small town in Ocean County, New Jersey, which is heavily republican. But, amazingly enough, many volunteers came to help our little campaign, though I think most did because of a hatred of Bush rather than strong supporters of Kerry. Kerry was a good candidate who happened to run an awful campaign. I'm sure books will be written about errors the staff made, primarily not responding to the lies of the swift boat hacks of Rove. I was also very disappointed in Kerry when he said he would have supported the war even after he knew that there were no WMD's. This was a major mistake that I believe he never recovered from. But that was then, and here we are now.

As a student of history, it is my belief that this administration will go down as the worst in our 200 years as a nation. I used to think that Nixon was the most corrupt, but at least the EPA, Clean Air and Clean Water Acts were passed during his years. This arrogant bunch of liars and profiteers are in position to absolutely ruin this country. The list of what they have done to us could fill a book, but to list a few: huge tax cuts to the very wealthy at the expense of the middle and lower classes; the rape of the environment on every front, which could take decades to repair if ever; a bankruptcy bill that protects credit card companies that give out cards like candy and throws more people into economic ruin; and finally, an illegal war against a nation that did nothing to this country or its neighbors.

After the first Gulf War, neocons like Rumsfeld, Wolfowitz, Cheney, and others planned for years to eliminate Saddam Hussein from Iraq to obtain the second largest deposit of oil in the world. Paul O'Neill and Richard Clarke have written that this was the first order of business after the empty suit from Texas took office. When 9/11 happened, they had their excuse to carry out plans that had been brewing for 10 years. Even when told that there was no evidence linking Saddam to 9/11, it didn't matter. They knew after that tragic day the American people could be bamboozled into anything with the name of security for the homeland on it. As the Downing Street Memo accurately tells us, "the intelligence and facts were being fixed around the policy." Many of us knew this long before the bombing started. We marched in the streets; we wrote letters to our representatives and editorial pages in the papers; and we signed petitions. And we were called unpatriotic by the right wing nuts in power. Is this any way to run a democracy? They want a democratic nation is Iraq, all the while destroying our own.

I despair for our country. Money runs the place and taking more from the middle class for their wealthy friends and industries has become the national past time. Religious zealots want to install a theocracy, and those who don't believe in the same nonsense as they do will burn in hell. These same fundamentalists are taking over the schools in the Midwest, and teaching the ridiculous notion of creationism and that science is not be trusted. Our students are already behind the next economic powerhouses of India and China; why are we allowing this to happen? Why are we so afraid of confronting these religious bullies?

The Democratic Party will continue to be the party out of power until they remember who they are, the party of FDR, JFK, and Bill Clinton. I can just imagine Bobby Kennedy spinning in his grave up on that hill in Arlington with what the Republicans have done to truth and justice for all. I was sick when they allowed the latest three right wing activist judges get approved without a filibuster. You know that if the positions were reversed, the GOP senators would have held out until hell froze over. The Dems have no discipline and it seems each goes his or hers own way. They must take a stand soon on Social Security, judges, the environment, and issues helping the majority of this country. Stand up for what they believe is best for all of us. Stand up for something.

Susan Puder has been a democratic activist for decades; a protector of the environment; has rarely met a Republican she likes; a former technology specialist who worked in NYC for years and on 9/11/01 experienced the fear of all in that city that day; a nature photographer; and can't wait for Bush to be out of office.

Then and Now

by Danna Kiel

When I was a kid and first learned of elections, democrats, republicans and all things political I thought it was like a board game. The United States was the board, as in Monopoly. We democrats, decked in blue, were the donkeys and the evil red republicans were elephants. My understanding of democrat vs. republican was as simple as "good vs. evil."

Blue was the color of good, the color of water. Red was the bad color of the devil and his pitchfork. Good should prevail—and it did, although I was disappointed that we were donkeys and they were elephants. In general, elephants are more respected than donkeys, save that it was an ass that Jesus rode into Bethlehem. As a child I wasn't certain if this was how the country should be run, but as long as the democrats won I guessed it was okay.

I did wonder, as a proud child democrat, what having the democrats running the country meant in terms of what the republicans wanted. It raised the question of just who knew best what to do for ALL people, a question I still ponder following the 2004 election. If some people had needs that our guy hadn't thought of, what then? This over-thinking soon became overwhelming for me and I dismissed it, since we won and that was all that mattered. The board game analogy seemed to work until I was old enough to register my first loss.

When Governor Ronald Reagan beat incumbent President Jimmy Carter by a landslide in the 1980 election I was devastated. It had never occurred to me, a politically astute 8th grader living in New Orleans, Louisiana, that we would or could lose. During responsive Morning Prayer at Epiphany, the parochial school I attended, Sister Cecilia blessed the winner by saying, "and for the newly elected President Ronald Reagan." Our response was supposed to be, "Lord, hear our prayer," but we said nothing and the room fell silent. After an immediate reprimand, there were some scattered "Lord, hear our prayers" heard throughout the room.

My father kept my twin sister and I aware of politics and current affairs, and even took us into the voting booth with him. He also took us to National Urban League convention meetings and the like when we were 12 years old. It was not until recently that I could appreciate how keenly aware of the turning tide my 8th grade class must have been not to respond to that Morning Prayer. Our 30-second protest was certainly not planned.

I was a Democrat long before I could vote, but why our party had the unthinking, unfeeling donkey as our mascot remained a mystery to me. As far as I could see we were a caring and sensitive group of people. My mother counted Lyndon Baines Johnson as her favorite president because he signed and enacted Civil Rights legislation set in motion by John F. Kennedy before his assassination. LBJ ended his famous address to the world with the unflinching words, "we shall overcome," a song lyric that had become not only a slogan but a call to action during the active days of Civil Rights protests. It was, however, Robert Kennedy—Attorney General in his brother's cabinet—that she counted among favorite politicians and legislators.

I came to understand her choice during my film studies as an adult. A screening of D.A. Pennebaker's film "Crisis," which documents the desegregation of the University of Alabama, opened my eyes to Bobby Kennedy's heroics. When Alabama Gov. George Wallace refused to allow two Black students to register for classes at the University of Alabama in 1963, the students had to be escorted by the Alabama National Guard, federalized as a result of the efforts of Bobby Kennedy. Wallace was stubborn, but despite his hubris and, most of all, his ignorance, change came.

What I know now is that "Democracy" describes how our government runs and that we in fact live in a republic, a republic of united states. Although "Democracy" and "Democratic" find their etymology in the same word, the first is a noun that defines our way of life in America and the other an adjective that defines partisan affiliation connected with specific values, concerns and philosophies that have existed over time or developed according to what is important to the group, our group. The terms, although not mutually exclusive as some might think, are not synonymous either.

Being a Democrat is more than a political choice; it is, I believe, a spiritual one. Democracy is more than a way of government; it is a pervasive spirit. We who inhabit the Blue States are not merely ruled by the principles and tenants of this form of government, we are bound by it. In America, Democracy is the air we breathe. Children know the concept before they can define or even say the word.

Democracy in America means our government is comprised of officials elected by the people from amongst the people. We must, however, cease to assume ourselves a mass of people herded behind one shepherd. It does not matter whether he is the shepherd of our choosing or someone else's. Such dependence places our inherent power at the whims of forces we cannot control. We will always find ourselves forlorn and powerless if we look without instead of within.

I certainly count engaging, emerging and established leaders like Barack Obama, Al Sharpton, Maxine Waters, John Conyers, John Kerry, John Edwards, Hillary Rodham Clinton, Barbara Boxer and Rev. Jesse Jackson as continued blessings to not only African Americans, other minority communities, residents of the Blue States, but all states. We must now look to them (and others like them) as inspiration and catalysts for our own action. Those of us who can must educate ourselves, observe the world outside our window and use technology and its tools to remain current, aware and sensitive to our precious planet. Like Marvin Gaye, we must constantly ask the question, "What's Going On?"

We must imagine ourselves leaders of our households, communities, cities and states, our country and the free world. We must also believe ourselves masters of our fates, captains of our own destinies. We must continue to believe in dreams: our parents', our own and our children's. We must see ourselves as agents of change.

Our imperative is to believe in our own transformation. As Sen. Obama has stated, "Democrats have to say to themselves, 'What are the values we care most deeply about?' then do the hard spiritual work ahead of time. You can't every once in a while just throw in the word 'God'." (Newsweek's "Who's Next Issue" Jan 3, 2005 p 82)

Our gaze must be fixed on our own evolution, as well as a return to the core values of the party—family, community, and faith—that according to Obama were rejected by some in the party during the 1960's. Democrats lost their bid for the White House as well as numbers in Congress. Our faith and our hope, however, must be placed in our collective and respective God, the Higher Power that is our beginner and our finisher. This Higher Power lives within all of us, therefore making us power-full.

I reflect on my childhood musings of all things red and blue, donkeys vs. elephants and good vs. evil and I understand that animals and colors don't really matter now. The Democratic Party is our choice; a better world is our mandate. As a mother, an African American woman, and a filmmaker I am responsible to my son and the future of his world. His future, our future, begins today.

Danna Kiel is a journalist and, as mentioned above, a filmmaker and proud single parent. She currently resides in the blue state of California.

Red State Values: Rhetoric versus Reality

by Michael McFadden

Most analysts reported that the 2004 election was decided by a massive influx of voters who were concerned with, and based their choice for President on, values issues. Of these issues, objection to abortion, and gay marriage were of paramount concern to these voters. The one thing that ties these two issues together is their alleged impact on our nation's supposed moral compass.

While this connection is tenuous (at best) due to the unlikelihood, if not inability, of Gay couples to have unwanted pregnancies and seek abortions, we must nonetheless concede that the private sexual lives of our citizens does impact, or perhaps awaken from centuries of a 'VanWinkle-like' slumber, our national moral compass. Pretty hard to look at a history book and discern when, if at all, our nation actually had a moral compass, but with an eye to the 60's, I will concede the point and move on.

On every stop during the 2004 campaign, the President went to great lengths to proclaim his faith, and often contrasted his faith with that of his opponent. The United States professes to be a mostly Christian nation, and this (Christianity) is where the President and his supporters demonstrate the disconnect between the religious dictates of their professed faith and the policies they actually pursue. The religious dictates of Christianity, as espoused by God's chief spokesperson (Jesus Christ) and his assigned lawgiver (Moses), are at odds with the political dictates of today's Republican Party.

The problem for conservative Republicans is that the book that expresses God's dictates on all mankind—the Bible—has already been written. Once something has been written, its text speaks for itself, and discrepancies (if any) only arise as to the interpretation of said written text. Where the text, and the context into which it was delivered, are clear and unambiguous (as in the sermon on the mount), the reader/worshiper are entitled to rely on the plain meaning (dictionary) of said words. As a result, the Republicans are faced with a serious, yet incredibly well managed political problem.

While Jesus Christ never addressed those issues which get Republican panties all in a bunch (abortion, homosexuality/Sponge Bob, etc.), he made over 80 references to the poor, and the most vulnerable in our society. Unfortunately for the Son of God, providing for the sick and the poor requires a level of taxation that is, while consistent with the needs of a growing segment of Republican voters, fundamentally inconsistent the low-tax orthodoxy of the party leaders. This is reminiscent of the misdirection wealthy (red state) plantation owners used to get poor and uneducated southern whites to fight in the Civil War. These poor, illiterate and long-suffering individuals were cleverly convinced to fight to preserve an institution (slavery) in which they had no stake. In a bit of historical 'deja-vu,' Republicans mislead red state whites to vote against their own financial best interest in favor of their cherry-picked biblical mandates.

The disconnect between the teachings of Christ, and the Republican's low-tax orthodoxy, places those who claim to legislate with an eye toward their faith in a factually and rhetorically, though not politically, untenable situation. These Republicans reason, or at least argue (stealthily), that because there are biblical figures who speak to the issue of homosexuality, their opposition to its' practice is rooted in biblical text. These Republicans come well armed with biblical references and quotes, which initially seem to render their positions unassailable. However, upon closer examination (which almost never happens) it becomes clear that they have engaged more in biblical cherry-picking then actual textual analysis.

A fitting analogy would be judging the great Chicago Bulls teams by focusing on the actions of Dennis Rodman, rather than those of Michael Jordan. Not to elevate Dennis Rodman to the status (morally or otherwise) of a biblical figure, but the acknowledged star of the Bulls was Michael Jordan, and the acknowledged star of the Bible is Jesus Christ. Thus, any analysis of the Bulls must begin with Michael Jordan, and any analysis of the Bible must begin with the teachings of Jesus Christ. Facing this threat to their low-tax orthodoxy, the Republicans basically write Jesus Christ out of his starring role in the Bible! To do this, they quote (cherry-pick) directly from the Bible as the foundation of their moral outrage, while simultaneously ignoring the teaching of God's only son! As a result, they are able to cast themselves as the guardians of morality, and their political opponents as the protectors of a secular, godless culture.

This "Christ-lite" form of Christianity was nearly brought to its' knees last year when the current Governor of Alabama asked the legislature to raise taxes to pay for better schools and other government services. The Governor, a former Republican Congressman, stated that as a member of congress he never saw a tax cut he didn't vote for, but as the state's chief executive, his priorities had changed. Upon taking office the Governor toured the state and found that his poorest residents (some without indoor plumbing) were paying a higher percentage of their annual income in taxes than were his more affluent residents (many with swimming pools). He petitioned the legislature to raise taxes, and informed his opponents that taking care of the needy was their "Christian" duty. The same "devout Christians" who threw themselves into fits of prayer in protest over the removal of a stone plaque depicting the Ten Commandments (graven image), nonetheless soundly rejected the Governor's appeal to put their faith into practice. Needless to say, there was no tax increase!

This phenomenon is most clearly demonstrated by the debate over abortion. Imagine trying to win a values debate with someone who declares their position as pro-life! Where Democrats fail their supporters (and themselves) is that they do not challenge the Republicans on how they characterize their position. Are they really pro-life, or are they simply "pro-birth?"

Their low-tax orthodoxy is in direct conflict with encouraging a culture of life (and Jesus's requirement that Christians provide for the poor) in that they are unwilling to fund any programs that make life worth living! How can they be pro-life and simultaneously reject Head Start, childhood immunization, and a host of other programs that help ensure that there is quality in one's life? Can their moral focus be so narrow as to require birth with no corresponding obligation as to providing for the quality of the lives they would require to be brought to full term? To be sure, our nation's laws recognize this connection as evidenced by the bevy of "quality-of-life" legal requirements the laws of all 50 states impose on parents. In the absence of these life sustaining programs, our poorer citizens (those about which Christ spoke) are subjected to lives mired in poverty.

Most aborted babies are, for financial and other reasons, unwanted and would likely be treated as such if their births were legally mandated. It seems that one could reasonably argue that if your parents don't want you, they are not likely to raise you in an environment of love and support. In a country where 90% of our correctional inmates were both undereducated (most have not graduated from high school) and poor, it is illuminating to note that crime dropped precipitously 18 years after the passage of Rowe V. Wade! Children who weren't wanted weren't born, and thus their likely troubled childhoods did not result in likely criminal behavior. While it is pretty difficult to fail to see this connection, Democrats fail to make it, and a pliable and naive red state electorate embraces the unchallenged values rhetoric of the Republicans.

The ability of the Republicans to rewrite established text is not limited to religious documents. The Second Amendment of the US Constitution specifies that the right of the citizens to keep and bear arms is subject to the establishment of, and citizen participation in, a well-regulated militia. In their zeal to argue that the Second Amendment provides for unlimited access to guns (gun manufacturers and the massive gun lobby are huge Republican campaign contributors), the Republicans have basically replaced the comma prior to the well regulated militia phrase (a qualifier to the right to bear arms) with a period, thus transforming that qualifying phrase into a meaningless sentence fragment! Again, their modus—operandi is the same. They seize a position based on the cherry-picked text of a sacred document, argue that they are the true guardians of said text, and then rely on a pliable, naive, and uninformed red state electorate to support them at the polls.

While the uninformed-ness of the electorate is crucial to the Republicans' success, it is the most fragile ingredient in this political misdirection because it is the one element not solely within their ability to control (Armstrong Williams et al notwithstanding). A pliable, naive, and uninformed electorate cannot exist without a pliable, naive, and uninformed press, and a rhetorically challenged, and de-boned (backbone) opponent! Democrats fail themselves and their constituents by virtue of their inability to hold Republicans to the requirement that their values rhetoric matches their reality.

Michael G. McFadden, or Sherman and Barbara's baby boy (as he sometimes refers to himself) is an attorney, writer, political junkie, local activist, and lifetime resident of Baltimore City.

Reclaiming Democracy: People versus Markets

by Jay R. Mandle

You may or may not know the name Grover Norquist. But if you do not, you should. Norquist is the president of the innocuous-sounding Club for Growth. But his official position with that organization does not begin to suggest the reach of his power as an ideologue and organizer of the political Right. As Bill Moyers says of Norquist, "unofficially he's been the linchpin in Washington for the conservative revolution that now controls the government."[1]

What is it that Norquist wants? According to Michael Scherer, a journalist who profiled him in Mother Jones, Norquist's goal is "an America in which the rich will be taxed at the same rates as the poor, where capital is freed from government constraints, where government services are turned over to the free market, where the minimum wage is repealed, unions are made irrelevant, and law-abiding citizens can pack handguns in every state and town." Less gently, and in his own words, Norquist says he wants to "get it [government] down to the size where we can drown it in the bathtub."[2] Not surprisingly, Norquist has little to say about the role of private money in politics and what little he does have to say argues against campaign finance reform.[3]

What is alarming about all of this is that Norquist is so influential in the Bush White House. Indeed, Ralph G. Neas, president of People for the American Way, underlines the point. According to Neas, "If the American people really

---

1. Now with Bill Moyers, Transcript: Bill Moyers Interviews Grover Norquist, October 10, 2003. http://www.pbs.org/now/transcript/transcript norquiest.html.
2. Michael Scherer, "The Soul of the New Machine," MotherJones.com, January/February 2004 Issue
3. "Selected Statement from New Hampshire Press Conference on the McCain-Feingold Campaign Finance Reform Bill." http://www.atr.org/issues/cfr/092399-c.html.

want to know what George W. Bush is up to, the best place to look is the candor of Grover Norquist."[4] This is most explicit in the Bush Administration proposals to create private accounts to pay for health and retirement benefits. It is therefore no joking matter when Norquist says: "My ideal citizen is the self-employed, homeschooling IRA-owning guy with a concealed-carry [gun] permit...because that person doesn't need the goddamn government for anything".[5]

This is a call for a radical counter-revolution. Since the advent of industrial capitalism in the nineteenth century, the government has been the institution to which vulnerable and politically aroused populations have looked to protect their interests. They do so when market forces produce intolerable outcomes. These come in many different forms. Markets, unregulated by the government, do not ensure safe working conditions or environmental protection. They do not adequately supply sanitation facilities, prevent child labor or offer adequate levels of education to the population. It is the government, not the market, that historically has provided bulwarks against discrimination, has mitigated poverty in old age, and has facilitated the right to collective bargaining. Markets of course can and do satisfactorily make consumer goods available. But there is a long list of services that the government has to supply and an equally long list of policies that must be in place if market failures are to be corrected. Acceptance of the Norquist agenda of minimizing government means reversing the victories won by citizen movements to overcome the negative social consequences of market failures.

Norquist is not entirely wrong when he says that his opponents "want to use the government to bring money and power to themselves." But when he characterizes the people who benefit from governmental interventions as "parasites" his intentions are made clear.[6] The government as a countervailing institution to market domination is to be gutted.

According to Norquist, the coalition that has successfully moved politics to the Right is housed in the Republican Party and is composed of tax payers, property owners, small business people and members of communities of faith. What unites them, he writes, is that "they want to be left alone." They want low taxes, the elimination of regulations, free trade and a prominent role for their religious

---

4.   Quoted in Michael Scherer, "The Soul of the New Machine."
5.   Quoted in Michael Scherer, "The Soul of the New Machine."
6.   Frontline, "Interview Grover Norquist," September 2, 2004. http://www.pbs.org/ wgbh/pages/frontline/shows/choice2004/interviews/norquiest.html.

beliefs. What makes this coalition work and "the reason the modern Republican Party holds together" is that, as Norquist reports, "it is a low-maintenance coalition." What unites the members of the coalition is their shared desire to role back government programs.[7]

Norquist can hardly contain his glee when he looks at the composition of the Democratic Party. What he sees there—environmentalists, feminists, reformers, big city political machines, civil rights activists, unions and trial lawyers—is disarray. Unlike the coalition he is building, Democrats do not agree on a clear overarching objective. Democrats have no conception comparable to Norquist's idea that he is building a "leave-us-alone" coalition.

There are obvious problems in Norquist's analysis. It is difficult, for example, to maintain that the religious components of the conservative coalition really are content to be "left alone." Theirs is a much more aggressive agenda, which hopes to impose a specific morality on the country as a whole, and they would not be reluctant to employ governments in this endeavor. Similarly, very substantial tensions lurk within the conservative movement over foreign policy. Norquist himself views the Iraq war with great skepticism, fundamentally because it necessitates an expansion of the role of the government. But obviously other elements of the coalition, particularly centered in the administration itself, disagree.

Nevertheless, there is not much to be gained in pursuing an assessment of the internal tensions within the conservative coalition or to speculate on the question of how long it can remain intact. For the fact is that the recent trend to the radical Right has deep-seated sources in American culture and society. Even if the Republican coalition falls on hard times, the attractiveness of a politics that calls for a dismantling of the government will continue to possess resonance. Reversing the trend to the Right will require a political alternative that finds and cultivates the same kind of cohesion that empowers the Norquist coalition.

At issue, fundamentally, is the question of the government. The political Right has taken advantage of the belief present among large segments of the American people that the government is an enemy. As John R. Hibbing and Elizabeth Theiss-Morse have written, "except for an occasional interlude, such as when the country needs a rallying point in the wake of a serious outside threat,

---

7.   Frontline, "Interview with Grover Norquist."

the American public has not had much trust in their government for the past thirty years."[8] Convinced that the government is untrustworthy, there is no place for voters to turn but to the market in seeking redress for their problems. Before the political tide to the Right can be reversed therefore, something will have to be done to resuscitate a belief in the effectiveness of the government in protecting the people's interests. If voters are to be convinced that the market is not the solution to all of society' ills and inadequacies, they will have to be persuaded that the government is capable of advancing their interests.[9]

Survey data suggests that the basis for the public's aversion to the government is closely tied to the issue of private money in politics. People believe elected officials serve only special interests.

Hibbing and Theiss-Morse write that data collected by the Gallup Organization in 1998 indicate that "the unholy union of elected officials and special interests is easily the most despised aspect of the American political system."

They report that 77 percent of respondents agreed that "special interests had too much control over what government does." What is interesting in this regard is that the problem the American people seem to have with the government and politics generally does not concern the social policies that actually have been adopted. Rather, according to the authors, "what bothers them is decisions made for the wrong reasons—out of a desire on the part of politicians to secure gifts, campaign contributions, trips to Tahiti and lucrative post-governmental-service private-sector positions from special interests rather than out of a desire to act in the general interests of real Americans." Hibbing and Theiss-Morse write that "our survey and focus group results indicate that people are convinced the political system as it operates today allows self-interested decision makers to confer additional benefits on themselves by the decisions they make even as they are already drawing (ostensibly) lavish salaries and benefit packages from the taxpay-

---

8.   John R. Hibbing and Elizabeth Theiss-Morse, "What Would Improve Americans' Attitudes Toward Their Government?" Paper prepared for presentation at the Conference on Trust in Government, Princeton University, November 30-December 1, 2002, p. 1.

9.   See Marc J. Hetherington, <u>Why Trust Matters: Declining Political Trust and the Demise of American Liberalism,</u> (Princeton: Princeton University Press, 2005) for more on this.

ers they ignore" and that "the people, feeling used, absolutely detest this style of decision making and are willing to do virtually anything to avoid it."[10]

With attitudes like these, it is easy to understand the responsiveness of the American people to the siren call of right-wing market fundamentalism. What is promised is an escape from the corruption of the political process. In its place is a vision of individual gain through market participation. The sales pitch is that by substituting, for example, private accounts for traditional social security, an individual's economic well-being will be advanced in ways that a corrupt political process could not deliver. The strength of the pitch is rooted in the promise of market participation without the involvement of politicians. Never mentioned, of course, are the serious risks associated with market participation, the fact that markets do not provide anything to people whose incomes are too low for them to be effective participants, and that many services that people need can only be provided by the government, not by profit-seeking firms.

No one knows the extent to which the gains secured in the 2004 election by the Bush Administration were the product of the attractiveness of the Right's anti-government stance. It might just as well have been the product of war-induced solidarity. But in its second term the Bush Administration has already moved to enhance the role of markets in both the social security and the health care systems. The support for the Administration generated by the war will likely provide the cover the Administration needs for it to try to implement its market agenda.

If this agenda is implemented, however, the results are bound to disappoint the American people. The fact is that the Right has seriously exaggerated the ability of markets to solve social problems. But even as the inadequacies associated with increased reliance on markets become obvious, it by no means certain that voters will choose to reverse direction and endorse government programs to meet their needs. For the American people's antipathy to the way politics is engaged in will almost certainly persist even as they learn that markets are not panaceas. The electorate will then be caught between its mistrust of the government on one hand and the fact that, on the other hand, only government can effectively address many of society's needs. With this the case it is no sure thing that voters

---

10. John R. Hibbing and Elizabeth Theiss-Morse, "What Would Improve Americans' Attitudes Toward Their Government?" p. 8, 9.

will turn to government programs as an alternative to markets. Instead, the electorate is likely to believe it confronts two choices, both of which are unattractive: corrupt government or markets insensitive to people's needs.

In this perspective it is possible to see not only the structural weaknesses of the Democratic Party but also the potential that exists for its renaissance. The party is, as Norquist puts it, the party of government. At its best, it is the party that supports enhanced social programs that speak to the needs of the overwhelming majority of the American people. The social security system, which has become remarkably effective in reducing poverty among the elderly, is an important case in point. Thus, it is possible that voters might turn to the Democrats when the Right's market reliance becomes a demonstrable failure. But at the same time precisely because it is the party of government, Democrats suffer more than the Republican Party or Norquist-type conservatives from the electorate's skepticism concerning the motives of politicians. The problem that faces the Democratic party is that while it is the source of the social policies that stand as an alternative to those of the political Right, it is the victim of the wide-spread belief that government cannot be trusted because politics is corrupt and corrupting. To the extent that voters act on their antipathy to government, Republicans can expect to be the beneficiaries; if however that mistrust can be overcome, then the Democratic Party could again become the governing party.

The aversion to government and politics is not a problem only for Democratic Party candidates. Everyone advocating reform confronts the same roadblock. Whatever the issue—not only health care and social security but the environment, poverty, discrimination, worker rights, minority rights—when reformers advocate governmental interventions and non-market solutions, the role of money in politics leads the American people to a cynical pessimism. This is because it is very hard to argue convincingly that a political process funded by private wealth will produce superior outcomes so than markets in which that same private wealth is dominant.

Promoting the public funding of elections is the obvious way out of this trap. With a "clean money" system a persuasive argument can be made that that government has the potential to be something other than a tool used by campaign contributors. Indeed, this is the argument that has to be made convincing if voters are to be wooed away from their conviction that the political process is dysfunctionally corrupt.

Fortunately, the "clean money" experience in Maine and Arizona can be used to bolster the argument. In those states full public funding is provided for candidates for statewide office. The result has been that politics has become more democratic (not necessarily a capital D). Political office seekers are now much more representative of the population as a whole because wealth or access to wealth no longer is the most important criterion that has to be satisfied to be a viable candidate. Just as important, the experience in those states suggests that a clean election system advances a non-market agenda. State policies in both states have advanced governmental assistance in health insurance and prescription drug policy. We now have enough practical experience with a "clean" system to convincingly argue that it works.

But "clean elections" have not been endorsed by the leadership of the Democratic Party. The public funding of candidates was adopted in Maine and Arizona by voters in referendums, not by Democrats in legislatures. Indeed, Democrats in the Massachusetts legislature destroyed the clean money system the voters voted for. It is true that Democrats more than Republicans did support McCain-Feingold (the Bipartisan Campaign Reform Act, BCRA). But their flouting the clear intent of BCRA by raising millions of dollars through unregulated 527s dissipated whatever good will the party might have earned as the party of campaign finance reform by their votes. Democrats have not altered the perception or the reality that their party, as well as the Republican party, is a vehicle by which big financial donors control politics.

Indeed, the Center for Responsive Politics reports that in the 2004 election cycle Democrats running for federal office (House, Senate, as well as President) raised more money than did Republicans. And while the role played by small donors in Democratic Party fund-raising was somewhat more important than was the case for Republicans, the fact remains that for both parties contributions of over $200 represented the bulk of the funds raised.[11] What is significant about this is the tiny fraction of the population that such large contributors represented. Less than 0.5% percent of the adult population made contributions of $200 or

---

11.   During the 2004 electoral cycle the Democratic Party raised 71.2 percent of its funds from donors who contributed more than $200. The comparable figure from the Republicans was 84.5%. Computed from Center for Responsive Politics, 2004 Election Overview: Stats at a Glance and Donor Demographics http://www.opensecrets

more. There really is very little to choose between the major parties with regard to the way they fund themselves.

All of this might be understandable and less damaging to Democrats if they defended this dependence on private funding and questionable ethics as a necessity, required in order to compete in the current system, while at the same time promising to change the system once they were in office. But in fact the presidential website for John Kerry made no mention whatever of the issue of campaign finance reform. Further, Senator Edward Kennedy's recent speech to the National Press Club, celebrated as a vision for Democrats, failed to mention the role of private wealth in politics as a problem to be solved.[12] The Democrats, in short, are in denial. They do not recognize that as the party of government they more than the Republicans are victimized when the electorate expresses its skepticism about how the political process functions.

But the evidence of that victimization is unambiguous. John Kerry's 48% of the vote pales compared to the 61% received by Lyndon Johnson in 1964. Today there are 44 Democrats in the Senate compared to 61 in 1977. The number of Democrats in the House now is 202; in 1977 that number 292. There are now 22 sitting Democratic governors compared to 36 in 1975. And in 2003 there were 16 state legislatures controlled by Democrats. In 1975 that number was 30. The trend is clear and so are its consequences. Because of the decline of the Democratic Party, we are moving towards a situation in which wealth more than ever rules, and public programs to offset the harsh edge of markets will be reduced in scope or eliminated.[13]

It is hard to see how the Democrats can reverse this trend unless they first provide a reason for the electorate to believe that government and politics are not inherently corrupt. That, in turn, is all but impossible to envision unless and until the Democrats become the party of "clean government." This is not as far-

---

12.   Ted Kennedy, "A Democratic Blueprint," Speech to the National Press Club, January 13, 2005. http://www.tompaine.com/print/a_democratic-blueprint.php.

13.   Data on the presidential election computed from "Elections 2004, Comparing 2004 with 2000. http://www.washingtonpost.com; Data on The Congress: Statistical Abstract of the United States 2003, Table 405, p. 261 and Infoplease, http://www.infoplease; Data on Governors, Statistical Abstract 2003, Table 412, p. 265 and The Green Papers: General Election 2004, http://www.greenpapers.com; Data on state legislatures, Statistical Abstract of the United States, Table 414, p. 267.

fetched as it might sound. We know from polling data that many if not most self-identified Democrats support schemes to reduce the role of private money in elections.[14] Though the party leadership has not moved in that direction, there is a significant constituency among Democrats that would welcome such a system.

The analogy is far from perfect, but in many ways today's Democratic Party faces a situation similar to the one the party confronted with the rise of the civil rights movement in the 1950s and 1960s. Then, as now, the party was populated by large numbers of individuals sympathetic to the cause of reform. But then, as now, the leadership of the party failed to take on the reform cause as its own. The Democrats of that era were very heavily dependent upon the white southern vote and were reluctant to risk alienating that constituency in the name of justice. The analogue today is that the party is reluctant to change the way elections are financed because its incumbents have mastered the art of political fund-raising.

What happened in the 1960s is well known. Outside of the confines of the party, a social movement, led in large part by young people, mounted a direct action campaign to dramatize the inequities of segregation. The student movement energized the adult Afro-American community and the two acted together to put pressure on liberals in the Democratic party to pass the path-breaking civil rights law of 1964 and the voting rights act of 1965. In effect, what happened was that the civil rights movement created a moral and political crisis to which Democrats (with a handful of Republican allies) were forced to respond with a legislative initiative.

A similar scenario not only is required but is also possible today. Again the Democrats are the gatekeepers of progressive social change. Democratic legislators are the most important and most likely decision-makers to be moved to support "clean elections." But that will not occur until pressure comparable to that experienced during the Civil Rights movement is directed toward them. The group that has to be moved is office holders who as incumbents possess a vested interest in the current system. They have to be pressured to change their position.

---

14.   A recent national poll indicated that 43.3% of adults who intended to vote for John Kerry strongly favored the public funding for candidates for state wide-office, while 28.5% of those who intended to vote for George W. Bush did so. See Public Campaign and Common Cause Survey by EDK Associates. Nationwide poll of 1000 adults (874 Registered voters) conducted October 2-23, 2004 by Opinion Research Corporation as part of their Caravan Omnibus survey.

The possibility that such pressure might be mounted exists because the inability of markets to resolve social problems is already becoming clear. Survey data consistently report in recent years that people do not agree when asked if they believe the country is headed in the "right direction."[15] But so far this recognition has not resulted in the public's endorsing Democratic-sponsored governmental interventions. But this is not likely to occur so long as the electorate believes that the political process is inherently tainted by the role of private wealth. Put another way, reforming the way electoral campaigns are financed is the first hoop that must be passed through if we are to initiate a new era of progressive governmental policies.

The current system of private funding of electoral efforts has inflicted a great deal of damage on attitudes towards government, too much damage for "clean elections" to be an easy sell. By now any use of tax money is suspect, and the argument that tax money should be used to support politicians often evokes skeptical derision. But the Democratic Party leadership's reluctance to endorse "clean elections" is ultimately self-defeating. So long as that refusal persists, Democrats will be unable to overcome a major cause of the decline in their party's fortunes.

But there may be an opening to change such as the one experienced in the 1960s. What it would take, as it did in the earlier era, is a vibrant social movement—this time focused on "clean elections"—that would strengthen the position of advocates of reform within the party. That is the Democracy Matters project. Our task is to build a movement that will transform the Democratic Party into the party of "clean government." When accomplished two self-reinforcing processes will be underway. The Democrats' own electoral prospects will be enhanced and that in turn almost certainly will produce a new era of creativity in governmental programs.

---

15. Polls taken by the Los Angeles Times, NBC News/Wall Street Journal, Pew Research Center for the People and the Press, and the Gallup Organization all agree that since early 1999 there has been a dramatic decline in this measure. For example, according to the Gallup Poll in early February 1999 71% of adults reported that they were satisfied "with the way things are going in the United States at this time. That perception was reported as 46% in January 2005. PollingReport.com, "Direction of the Country." http://www.pollingreport.com/right.htm.

Movements for reform like ours ultimately cannot win without legislation. Reforming the electoral system requires that Congress pass laws. Legislators must vote for "clean elections," and this despite the fact that, as beneficiaries of the current funding system, they have reason to stand in opposition. The Civil Rights movement can help us to understand how, notwithstanding these formidable obstacles, a social movement for "clean elections" can nevertheless succeed.

It is possible to envision just such a setting today. If a broad-based alliance were to be created of those who oppose the marketization of society, and if it exercised sufficient pressure on the Democrats, the party might be galvanized to move, both in its own and the society's interests, to reform the way election campaigns are financed in this country. If that were the case, then at long last an alternative to Grover Norquist's "let me alone" coalition would have been created. A countervailing power advocating a "clean money" system, housed in the Democratic party but responsive to those outside as well as inside the party, could halt and reverse the steady movement to the Right that has been our recent political experience.

The urgent task that faces reform activists then is to build a movement for a "clean money" electoral system. Such a movement has the potential to be wide and diverse. It can and should attract all who reject market fundamentalism. If such a movement prospers, it will become the laboratory in which diverse groups with a multiplicity of ideas learn to work with each other to build a better society for everyone.

Jay Mandle, Ph.D. is the W. Bradford Wiley Professor of Economics at Colgate University, as well as the treasurer of the Democracy Matters Institute, founded by National Basketball Association star Adonal Foyle. His commitment to the issue of money in politics is evident in his regular monthly editorial, Money On My Mind, appearing on the Democracy Matters website, www. democracymatters.org.

The World

Terrorism—Its Forms and Foibles

by Winnie Williams

The Presidential election campaign of 2004 brought forth heated discussions around the issues the parties felt strongly about. Both Republicans and Democrats felt it was to their advantage to do well espousing—or disagreeing with—the themes of Medicare; changes to Social Security; abortion; the Iraqi Invasions ("shock and awe": we get in—how do we get out?); gay and lesbian marriage; the outsourcing of American businesses to other countries, leaving many of our own people jobless; 9/11 with its consequent war in Afghanistan. In short: Terrorism, which has since popped up in various places around the world. One of the President's closest cohorts stated that if the Democrat were elected, there would likely be another terrorist attack. Logic?

As a matter of fact, terrorism takes various aspects and forms, so we of African-American ancestry—in light of slavery and all the forms of cruelty, brutality and, indeed, terrorism of which slavery was comprised—are well familiar with stories of terror out of our "ol' folks" past: beatings for little or no reason; lynchings; KKK activities, etc. My sister Sue tells me of a story Granny Winnie—foster grandmother for whom I was named—told of her own youth during slavery before the Civil War. She ran away, but they caught her and she was beaten. She ran away a second time, was caught and brought back again, this time receiving a more severe beating. Still, in time she ran away again, was caught again, but this time she was thrashed severely. Sue, who didn't like to be touched in anger, said "But Granny Winnie, if you knew you would get a beating, why did you keep running away?" Granny Winnie, then well into her seventies, said slowly and sadly, "Chile, I jes' wanted to be free."

Thinking of these and other inequities after 9/11, I jotted down some thoughts of home-grown terrorism, some of which follow:

My ancestors were kidnapped from Africa
And brought to this country in chains
Lodged in the filthy Holds of slave ships
Their bruised bodies filled with pain.

For during the harsh Middle Passage
From their Motherland to these waiting shores
They had to sleep spoon-fashion in their own excrement…
I cry for my People—how about yours?

On arrival in this new "White man's country"
(Discounting rights of Native people living here)
They were herded off to the "auction block"
Sold as slaves to highest bidders. Filled with fear
Of these strange, cruel men alleged to "own them,"
Who separated families, and sold them apart.
How could anyone be so inhumane?
Like creatures born without a heart.

They were taken away by these new "masters"
To a "home" far from loved African soil—
That abode most often a dilapidated hut—
"Good enough for Black slaves" bought for toil.

Blacks had their lives and loves stolen from them.
In this strange land, they'd no place to run;
And more: they were denied their own language—
Forced to learn an English dialect tongue.

Ol "massa," as they were taught to call him,
Along with his slave-driver/overseer,
Taught them the work that had to be done
From gray dawn 'til darkness was near.

My heart cries out for my People!
Forced to work all their lives for no pay!

They built up and beautified another man's land
As did their descendants for centuries of days.

And when our "old folk" were finally emancipated
No compensation for past labor was ever paid:
No homes, jobs, not even "40 acres and a mule"
And no apology for their mistreatment was ever made.

Still, we emerged from harsh bondage a strong people,
Having survived the worst abuse there could be
But the cruelty spawned by race hatred
Continued for more than another century.

Throughout all those years our folk did battle
To attain real justice and dignity;
Our Leaders spoke eloquently for us,
And we tried hard to achieve equality.

But the Crow and the Klan and the Counsels
Worked just as diligently as we
With lynchings, rapes, bombings against us,
To ensure that we couldn't breathe free.

Came a time in the turbulent 1960's, when
Some semblance of fairness emerged.
Segregation was struck down in public venues,
And laws denying Blacks the right to vote were purged.

So we, whose Ancestors' labor built this country,
Were happy that at last we were "in,"
For we dearly loved this land our fathers died for,
Despite all the troubles here we'd seen.

Hey! We thought we had finally made it.
We relaxed, and proceeded to dream

That now, at last, we are Citizens First Class!
But things are not always as they seem.

For today there are recurring indications
That some rights that we thought we had won
Per The Supreme Court Decision in 1954,
Are unraveling now, coming undone.

So in order to hold things together,
We may have to battle yet again,
To ensure that ALL people, regardless of race
Are treated fairly, with respect, not disdain.

America is this world's most powerful Nation
And is so regarded over all the earth.
It is therefore incumbent that the "moral" USA
Shows true regard for all human worth.

Winnie Williams has been a poet since the age of ten, and the editor's mother for a considerably shorter period of time. She resides in the blue state of New York.

America Is Due for a Change

by Clarence Johnson

George W. Bush, who I did not vote for, is a warmongerer. He forces the country into a war that we have no chance of winning. Did we not learn from Vietnam?

He's claiming it's a war against terrorism but he's not fighting terrorists, he's fighting citizens who are comfortable with their lifestyle, religion-wise, socially and maybe even economically. Osama Bin Laden, who we should be exhausting every avenue to capture and punish, is no longer mentioned in any of the president's speeches. Innocent men and women are being killed to satisfy this man's ego…and his father's.

In the next year or so, the United States will re-institute the draft to make up the number of soldiers we need to fight this unwanted war. The citizens, who voted for Bush and may have children, may live to regret their choice.

The economy, which normally prospers in wartime, has not improved. It shows no sign of ever turning around. Past history shows that whenever America was in a war, the economy was booming. Even during the Vietnam War, which was unpopular also, the economy picked up. There are no indications showing any uphill spirals. Unemployment is rising every month.

The jobs that were mostly Americans are being shipped out to other countries, such as India and Russia. He's making no attempt to keep our jobs at home. This will affect the future of our children and the way they must compete with the world.

Maybe it's time to close our borders like China did back in the 1920's. They refused to let any people inside their borders until they straightened out their problems. Now they are a world power. It's to the point that Americans are being despised all over the world. Why? Because of Bush's policies and the lack of respect we are given.

Back in the day Teddy Roosevelt believed you should 'speak softly, but carry a big stick'—and that was a form of respect. Everyone respected us, but now everyone is sticking it to us. If we must fight a war, let's go all out and hopefully save a few men and women.

The sad thing is that I see no one on the horizon to come to our rescue. No one talking about the important issues…prescription drugs and Medicare for seniors, social security benefits that will last, etc.

America is due for a change. The revolution will not be televised….

Clarence Johnson, an alumnus of Rutgers University, lives in the blue state of New Jersey with his wife and daughters.

Brutal Honesty Regarding the State of the World

by Katrina R. Martin

How do I begin to write what has been so wrong for centuries? President Bush embodies all that is wrong with capitalism. He is corrupt and makes decisions the masses must deal with. Other countries hate our guts. We Americans hate each other. So what is the point of all this, really?

We as African Americans never had a choice in this whole process from the beginning, anyway. We are still an impoverished people across the globe. So why are we so concerned with political parties when we know deep down within us that either side could truly care less of us?

America's problems go well beyond President Bush and the war on Iraq because they began before the country was conceived. It all boils down to the simple word of respect. If Europeans had respect for Africans and treated them the way they would want to have been treated, the world would not be in the state of affairs it is in today. And the reality is that those whom have benefited the most of slavery, economically and psychologically speaking, still do not respect Africans and Contemporary Africans, whose ancestors were enslaved. Bottom line: There are ancient skeletons in America's closet, like racism and true equality for all, that are being kept skeletons because those whom have been in power over the centuries are still in power today. They also know that the descendants of those whom died creating this country by force are due to just as much power as they have. And that really scares them because they wonder what would we do to them if we had the opportunity. Many Black Psychologists have created a term for this: "Ghosts of the Plantation."

These truths are public knowledge and no one seems to take them seriously. The masses choose to listen to the propaganda and lies. Nothing I'm writing right now is new news, which is the kicker for me because what we are seriously supposed to do?

I'm still debating law school. My plan is to eventually become a part of the legislature to change many of America's racist laws and truly work on the Constitution's liberty for all. But a man accused of rape just killed the judge who was covering his case, the court reporter and deputy in Atlanta. So this action has opened the floodgates for all the reasons why America's capitalistic society must come to an end. Surely we as a people can come up with something better than this. People are dying over this madness. And now government officials have the audacity to discuss reevaluating and revamping security and safety measures.

The problem with this entire way of thinking is that it is reactive rather than proactive. We for some insane reason enjoy dealing with individual problems of the European capitalistic system instead of the issue of European capitalism as a whole, which of course is the true problem. That's why I will not hurt my fingers by typing or your eyes by reading the list of infinite problems this system has. I will rather just discuss the system so that maybe the dialog will then get us inflamed enough to abolish it and replace it with a more utopian focused objective.

Racism plus greed plus slavery plus worldwide European superiority plus five centuries equals capitalism, which equals worldwide poverty, mass self-hatred and mis-education, environmental pollution and chaos.

Have you ever seen "The Matrix," with Keanu Reeves and Lawrence Fishbourne? I not only loved it but it hit a little too close to home for me because of the underlying theme. Do you by any chance remember the scene when Morpheus, played by Fishbourne, was captured and Agent Smith disclosed his true mission? The Agent revealed that his species thought that humans were destroying the planet because humans always devastate one area and move to another. And the sad reality is that this is all true because Europe's idea of slavery (torture and rape for centuries) and the colonization of the world put a major wrench in the cycle of life. Everyone knew what they were doing was wrong, but they started making excuses. The North and South had a Civil War and America was truly divided. But no one ever decided to change the system that was created to allow the wrongdoing.

Please do not get any of this confused: Slavery created America's wealth and capitalism is the system that allowed it.

Katrina R. Martin is a recent Hampton University print journalism graduate from Oakland, California. She is currently pursuing a career in entertainment with her group, Flawless, an up-and-coming singing, rapping and dancing duo who plan to change the music industry and work their way up. Look out for them!

Real Concerns: Neoliberalism and an Unsafe World

by William Calathes

While many people in the United States and throughout the world were, and continue to be, deeply troubled by the re-election of George W. Bush to a second term presidency, from one perspective, this re-election is merely the symptom of what has been a steady march towards a world dominated by corporate fascism. This march, always a concern of progressive people and all of humanity at every moment of our existence, has, over the course of the past two decades, taken on a deeper, more urgent reality as globalization and the protection of capital have entered into a new phase of world-wide injury, tyranny, and destruction. Historically, within this conceptualized framework, the re-election of George W. Bush is, in some respect, largely irrelevant, because the more critical structural changes brought about by globalization are what real concerns should be focused upon. And, although any one of hundreds of occurrences may be used as a jumping off point, the one chosen for purposes of this article occurred in December of 1984 because the high levels of direct death and injury were so severe and the destruction from that occurrence continues on today.

Former chairman of Union Carbide, Warren Anderson, was charged with culpable homicide as a result of the occurrences stemming from the night of December 2 to 3, 1984. During that night, a massive poisonous chemical cloud of methyl isocyandate gas was emitted from his pesticide plant in Bhopal, India that immediately killed almost 10,000 people. Today, it is known that over 20,000 have died, with 30 survivors dying every month. Union Carbide was deliberately negligent in the factory's location, design, operation, and maintenance as investigations revealed that Union Carbide had cut corners on safety, and had attempted to conceal or minimize its responsibility. More than a half million people filed a joint civil suit against Union Carbide for $3 billion but, in a type of plea bargain, the Indian Supreme Court dropped the criminal charges against

Anderson and ordered Union Carbide to pay $470 million in damages as "full and final settlement of claims." The factory was simply abandoned and today, over 20,000 people in the surrounding area rely on drinking water contaminated with chemicals that have seeped into the ground water from the plant, causing cancer and other diseases. Union Carbide had selected Bhopal, India as the site of its plant since safety regulations there were significantly more lax than in the United States and therefore its profit margins could be increased and its corporate capital protected and expanded.

This devastatingly tragic incident has come to symbolize the beginning of new age of a more potent form of globalized corporate deviance, and in some sense may be viewed as a precursor to 9/11. In the eyes of many around the world, the Bhopal disaster, and many similar occurrences around the world, has created the justifiable perception of the United States as one of the primary perpetrators of this kind of "profit-at-all-costs" behavior. It is a type of deviance that is a direct result of an economic and foreign policy that has promoted free trade with impunity. This neoliberal economic approach to the geo-political realities throughout the world has replaced the cold war as the driving force in international politics and has made the entire world, including the United States, quite unsafe. For, as the New World economic order has taken shape, a multiplicity of new forms of deviant organizational behavior, corporate and state-organized, have developed along with it. This newly emerging form of deviant behavior is wide-ranging and, among other things, corrupts free-market economies and the concepts of democracy, and threatens the real security of all people around the world. As globalization proceeds, and becomes more "successful," the twenty-first century is becoming dangerously haunted by the specter of new and more potent "criminal" arrangements that are resulting from the organization around capitalism's new imperialism and its driving need to protect and expand capital at all costs.

On a substantive and pedagogical level, there is a pressing need to extend the current limiting confines of criminology, criminal justice, and political science instruction to include the foundational realities behind the newly developed perils of the twenty-first century. These realities are not only left fully unexamined by the established and traditional funding sources of American academia, corporate media and most politicians, especially those who are running for the highest offices. Fundamentally, what should lie at the core of our current concerns about "security" is the pathologically link between current corporate behavior throughout the world and the economic and political agenda of the neoliberal imperialists who are forging alliances all in the name of "free-trade."

On the most basic level, these alliances assist in the protection of capital and the ever-increasing profit margins, and result in the increasing corporate domination of political decision-making as a system that is violating human values in its emphasis on privatization and deregulation of private industry and public services. Quite specifically, this is what is missing from the discourses in the academia and from current American political scene. For example, the fact that the Enron capitalists, "barons of bankruptcy," were more than willing to undermine democracy if that necessitated limiting employee wages and benefits is not the focus of the majority of academic inquiries, nor does it seem to be of major concern for anyone running for American political office. And, what is also missing from debate and inquiry is the notion that the Bush administration promoted and waged a continual genocide against the people of Iraq as a mechanism to extract and control that nation's oil reserves. In fact, it is becoming increasingly clear that the new world economic order's activities is replete with a multiplicity of examples involving criminal, civil, international, and human rights law violations that are broader in their scope, more potent in their effect, and more immune from any form of formal, or informal, sanction or control.

Neoliberalism and globalization contribute to the processes leading to misconduct by activating the criminogenic potential of economic, political, and cultural asymmetries, as well as by creating new asymmetries. These asymmetries cause deviance by furnishing opportunities for misconduct, by generating motives for actors to take advantage of such opportunities, and by weakening social and political controls. In response to this, this article offers a number of conceptual definitions of terms necessary for beginning discussions and also provides an introduction to how race and poverty are primary variables within the globalized deviance construction schema. Finally, general suggestions are provided as to the creation of a broad-based social justice response. The chief policy implication of this introductory analysis is that the recently unleashed forces of neoliberalism need to be reined in throughout the world and held in check, while American governmental policies ought to better shield the least privileged from the adverse affects of globalized deviance.

CONCEPTUAL CLARIFICATIONS

Globalization is extending the reach, intensity, and victimization of all forms of organizational deviance. With the advent and intense proliferation of globalization and the free flow of capital, many age-old questions have once again appeared. Promises of more freedom, prosperity, and happiness for a larger number of people have turned out to be chimerical. Economic and power inequalities have widened within and across nations during the last two decades, and corporate capital is becoming increasingly concentrated even as it is compared to governmental resources. Of the largest 100 economies in the world today, 51 are corporations. Moreover, the number of poor has reached unprecedented levels, as social welfare programs and safety nets have been reduced or abolished. Throughout the world enormous populations have become more vulnerable to exploitation and victimization and the powerful are solidifying alliances that help to facilitate this exploitation.

Within this context, to make sense of the apparent disparate cases of crimes, criminals, and opportunities, it is necessary to acknowledge that there is no universally accepted definition of globalized deviance. Most importantly, however, it must be noted that this type of organizational behavior includes corporate and governmental crimes. For purposes of this paper, therefore, "globalized deviance" refers to organizational cross-border misconduct that entails avoidable and unnecessary harm to society, and is similar to other kinds of acts criminalized in the countries concerned or by international law/or internationally recognized human rights precepts.

"Globalization" is another term that is often used without clear definition. In its simplest sense, it refers to a growing interconnectedness and multilateral linkages across national borders, a state of the world involving networks of interdependence at multicontinental distances. The linkages occur through flows and influences of capital and goods, information and ideas, and people and forces, as well as environmentally and biologically relevant substances (such as acid rain or pathogens). Globalism has several dimensions, such as economic, cultural, environmental, or military, not all of which take place at the same time, so whenever globalism increases and becomes more intense, we can speak of "globalization."

The term "criminogenic asymmetries" refers to structural discrepancies and inequalities in the realms of the economy, law, politics, and culture. Such asymmetries are produced in the course of interactions between unequal actors or systems with distinct features. All asymmetries contain some criminogenic potential. Durkheim, one of the most well known figures of criminology, for example, argues that deviance can not be eliminated, because we are, and always will be different from each other. Even in a society of saints, minor deviations would be considered serious offenses. In modern societies, crimes are those behavioral differences (asymmetries) that have been outlawed by legislative bodies. There is always the opportunity for powerful actors to victimize the less privileged (economic, political, and power asymmetries), although this potential is not always materialized. Criminal opportunities are not necessarily taken advantage of primarily because actors do not always seek to make use of illegal opportunities. They may not regard such action as appropriate (due to socialization, internationalization of norms), or fear of adverse consequences. The criminogenic potential is most likely to be activated when opportunities, motives, and weak controls are all present. Much of this then must be broadened out into the context of organizational deviance and globalization so a broader understanding of globalization theory and its unmet promises, as well as the concomitant proliferation and development of transnational corporations can be made.

Fundamentally, globalization theory holds that corporate encirclement of the planet will bring with it greater prosperity, peace, and ecological balance. Certainly, it is difficult to resist embracing such an enticing vision, especially when there are no readily apparent viable alternatives. In many respects, following the Cold War, traditional nation-states, including both high-tech industrial democracies and the multitude of Third Word governments, have grown weaker and less relevant. And growing nationalism and ethnic division leading to xenophobia, fundamentalism, fascist tendencies and war plagues the community of nations. This leaves corporate capitalists and leaders of the industrialized countries to present their neoliberal brand of globalization as inevitable and themselves as healers of the world's ills.

In the absence of coherent alternatives, the transnational corporations inexorably thrive in meeting their objectives. Increasingly flagless and stateless, global webs of production, commerce, culture and finance are constructed virtually unopposed. They expand, invest and grow, concentrating ever more wealth in a limited number of hands. They work in coalition to influence local, national, and international institutions and laws. And, together with the governments of home countries in Europe, North America, and Japan, as well as international institutions, such as the World Trade Organization, the World Bank, the International Monetary Fund, and increasingly, the United Nations, they are molding an international system in which they can trade and invest even more freely—a world where they are less and less accountable to the cultures, communities and nation-states in which they operate. Underpinning this effort is not the historical inevitability of an evolving, enlightened civilization, but rather the unavoidable reality of the overriding corporate purpose—the maximization of profits and the protection of capital.

Organizational deviant acts, once lying in the ineffective jurisdictions of nation states, and human rights abuses, once committed primarily by repressive governments, are increasingly carried out in the corporate interest. This is quite a development, but perhaps not such a surprising one. It must be remembered, for example, that although the Universal Declaration of Human Rights speaks eloquently to the need of individual rights and freedoms, it is remarkably silent when it comes to corporate crime. It must be remembered that the declaration was composed directly following major United States and European corporate collaboration with Nazi Germany. Nazi collaborators such as Ford, General Motors, Chase Manhattan Bank, Bayer and Volkswagen set the stage for later corporations as ITT and others helped overthrow democracy and install the Pinochet dictatorship in Chile and as numerous companies that supported South African Apartheid evidence. And, Union Carbide's record in Bhopal is a frequently cited study as well. Clearly, the incidence and severity of organizational deviance has grown remarkably as globalization proceeds, unchecked, unencumbered and free to create the necessary associations to continue their activity with even greater skill, success, and impunity, creating an ever-increasingly unsafe world for us all and impacting most directly on most of the world's most vulnerable populations.

RACE AND POVERTY

The emergence of globalized deviance has a direct and harsh affect on millions of people worldwide. Perhaps most significantly, however, neoliberalism and the conspiracy to control and expand capital affects many people of color, particularly those in the Southern Hemisphere, who because they do not have a sufficient amount of food to eat, suffer from unacceptable rates of malnutrition and disease. Ever-increasing numbers of such people face growing inflation while their governments, which used to subsidize some aspects of their marginal living, are urged to end subsidies for food and adopt a more market-oriented economic program. Many workers in these economies are trapped in poor working conditions with low pay. Women are often expected to do backbreaking farm and domestic work, with few rights or benefits. Yet many of the fiscal policies pushed onto developing countries and adopted in northern countries exacerbate the problem of the most marginal, while celebrating the wealth of the rich.

In the North as well, people of color often find themselves left farther and farther behind. Even when state and federal governments in the United States report budget surpluses, adequate housing for the growing number of working class families and homeless families, the repairing of the physical structures of schools that house low-income students of color, and social services or medical attention for those most in need are virtually ignored.

Sweatshops that employ people of color working as virtual slave laborers are tolerated even encouraged, as part of the New World trade. The public space people of color and marginal groups are most dependent on, whether it is public hospitals, schools, parks, or a social welfare system, is constantly attacked as inconsistent with the needs of capital and the market. These disparate conditions are directly related to globalization. Most certainly, other people are also under threats from the globalization process. In fact, if left unchecked, the foundations of democracy and capitalism may be in jeopardy.

The style of globalism advocated by the Bush administration has favored the free movement and protection of capital, while being at best indifferent and, at worse, hostile to the more place-dependent labor. It is the dual relationship of mobile capital and fixed, unorganized and unprotected labor that has created the conditions for capital to dominate. This has been greatly enhanced by the United States position toward organized labor and capital. While the Bush adminsitration has been aggressive in protecting capital both at home and abroad, it has encouraged both the weakening of organized labor and removing protections for workers.

While both Japan and Europe have aggressively pushed for globalism, each has been more willing to protect labor, the environment and certain markets, at least within their own borders. It is the United States that has consistently been the most radical on liberalizing capital and protecting it as it moves across borders, and the most hostile in protecting labor and fragile markets. Protecting labor expresses itself not only in strong unions and workers' benefits, but also in a strong social welfare system. The United States has purposely moved toward weaker labor unionism, as well as an anemic social welfare system. It has used the globalism it has advocated as justification for keeping workers' jobs insecure, and pay and benefits relatively low. Workers are told that advocating for benefits will cause capital to leave to another location in the country or the world where workers are willing to work for less and fewer benefits.

The United States, through the Bush administration, and the international organizations over which it has substantial influence, such as the International Monetary Fund, has continued to demand protection of capital and encouraged or tolerated the suppression of labor and the environment in weaker southern countries. Capital is actively being directed to markets with low wages, where workers are sometimes abused and labor organizations suppressed. Vulnerable workers and the environment, especially in the Southern Hemisphere are forcefully subsidizing the wealth this globalism is creating. This logic is then used to weaken the position of labor in the North, as we are required to compete with unorganized, suppressed labor in the South.

While sweatshops and slave labor may attract capital investments, the futures of poor African-American mothers in urban America or of Aborigine families in Australia when it comes to government assistance or education is not a bright one. United States-style globalism seeks to suppress social welfare systems and support for public expenditures that do not directly benefit the expansion of capital. The social welfare system and other public services, such as schools, social services in the North and food subsidies in the South, are supported through taxes, and taxes reduce short-term benefits to capital.

In the North, it is women and minorities who are most dependent on the public sector. These racial and gender correlations make it all the easier to attack the legitimacy of taxation for this purpose. Taxes are seen as undesirable because they reduce profits and interfere with the market. But the public (in the form of taxes) can only support the public space, including the welfare system. Those who cannot thrive in the market environment without assistance, especially if they are people of color, are seen as freeloaders and illegitimate.

Public purposes and civic goods, to the extent they are even recognized, are no longer to be achieved through public institutions but are to be privatized. The democratic vision associated with public functions is to be abandoned and seriously curtailed in favor of the ideal of efficiency. Moreover, there is an abiding belief that democracy must be limited because it interferes with the private decisions of market experts, thereby reducing wealth and capital. And anything that is perceived with interfering with the growth of capitalism, be it the social welfare system, labor unions, civil rights or government programs, and even funding for public higher education is being curtailed, while government policies and structure that protect capital, including the military, are enhanced.

Although proponents of this style of globalism purport to support democracy, it is only a role subservient to capital. In the United States, there is now only a soft encouragement to vote, while on the global matters that shape our everyday lives, average citizens have no say. No one can regulate commerce and the deregulation of it is made to appear both good and natural. Attention is drawn from the fact that the powerful organizations supported by this are in a conspiracy to protect and control the flow of capital. Unfortunately, there are no organizations of equal power to protect the interests of workers, racial minorities, the environment, women and children, or students of urban higher education institutions. Globalization has not just transformed the flow of capital; it has transformed the role of government and the meaning of citizenship.

Today, Americans are now brought together as consumers, but kept apart as citizens. The transformed role of government is not to protect citizens or the precious safety net of public space, but to protect the flow of capital. Today, there is an authoritarian vision where armies police people and nations, so capital might be free. This, then, is truly the emergence of a new and omnipotent form of globalized deviance. But while capital relies on government to do its bidding, people do have power—the only power remaining is the power to establish collective action.

SOCIAL JUSTICE ACTIONS AND NEEDS

Modern society, and modern America, especially under the presidency of George W. Bush, is very much a "toxic culture" founded upon social arrangements that encourage the deterioration of the environment and human health. One of the primary examples of a truly physical toxic environment existing in the world today remains in Bhopal, India where over 120,000 survivors of the Bhopal disaster are in desperate need of medical attention as a result of the criminal actions of Union Carbide two decades ago. Their chronic exposure-induced diseases include breathlessness, recurrent fever, back and body aches, loss of sensation of in limbs, fatigue, weakness, anxiety and depression. An overwhelming majority of the exposed people earned their living through hard labor and thousands of families are on the brink of starvation because the breadwinners are dead or too sick to work.

Bhopal is not an isolated event. There are slow and silent Bhopals occurring routinely in almost every part of the world. Corporations are responsible for indigenous populations disappearing, marine mammals declining, species loss accelerating, clean water becoming scarcer, forests dwindling, oceans' fisheries collapsing, productive topsoil diminishing, contamination by pesticides and industrial chemicals steadily growing and chronic diseases rising. Globalization has increased the profitability and destructive impact of systematic illegal activity and is the major threat to survival of the natural world. The global transfer of power from national governments to transnational corporations is a disaster for human rights, the environment, social welfare, agriculture, food safety, workers' rights, national sovereignty, and democracy.

Globalization is constructing a political and economic environment more conducive to the commission and concealment of heinous acts of deviance on the earth's people and environment. The inadequacy of codes and structures to check corporations and to keep officials accountable, along with a total lack of international mechanisms or will, has prompted globalization to result in the greater institutionalization of corporate deviance and perpetration of human rights abuses throughout the world. In the United States, Congress and state legislatures will not begin to put human rights front and center in its foreign policy without consistent pressure from the public. Building a movement for human rights and self-determination at home and abroad is a formidable task in the face of disproportionate influence of corporate money in American politics.

In the same vein, there must be an awakening within overall humanity to the stark realities of these times. Critically, such an awakening must lead to the mobilization of people, including victims, to confront not simply George W. Bush and his administration, but to define corporate deviance and human rights abuses and to begin to truly see and document the horrific realities. It must be remembered that the Universal Declaration of Human Rights calls upon *all* organs of society to protect and promote human rights everywhere. After all, we *all* live in this global world and must therefore begin to design collaborative efforts to fight to protect rights, prevent and/or investigate all harms, bring people and organizations to justice, end poverty, stop racism, and heal victims, in order to reclaim our humanity from all those, not just the few "front" people who are absconding with it.

William Calathes, J.D., Ph.D. is a professor of Criminal Justice at New Jersey City University. He and his daughter reside in the blue state of New York.

Dispatch from Darfur

by Jennifer Thomas

Just a few months ago, leaving my comfy digs in Bujumbura—yet another humanitarian hub—for the belly of the beast in Darfur, in western Sudan, seemed distant and far off. When I first "heard" about Sudan, I was a Crossroads Africa Volunteer in Kenya. I met a Sudanese man who wanted to take my naïve ass to the capital city of Khartoum where the waters of the blue Nile met the White Nile. At 19, this sounded like a very exciting idea. The airfare was astronomical and despite whatever dubious wishes of this man, I was not worth it…so Khartoum remained this never had memory.

Some 20 years later, I am writing this from my office/home in El Fasher in North Darfur. I am on temporary duty with US Agency for International Development's U.S. Office for Foreign Disaster Assistance. I am a Sr. Field Officer for their Disaster Assessment Response Team (DART) that has been sent out to respond to the humanitarian crisis of millions displaced as refugees in the neighboring country of Chad and internally displaced persons in Sudan.

Though I have become and old African hand, I was longing for a change from my lush green central African existence with the on-going, almost clockwork-like episodes of malnutrition, malaria, cholera and meningitis epidemics. Not that these things are not happening in Darfur, but it is happening in a different context and in a different culture, and the change is welcomed.

Darfur reminds me of Northern Senegal and Northern Mali. I realize that there is limited variation in a desert. It is hot with lots of sand. Men usually wrap themselves from head to toe, which would be the opposite approach to someone in the west, but if you know the sun like it shines here, you will understand that the layers of cloth are protection from the invasive and harmful rays. In the U.S., Minnesota can get 100 inches of snow and life goes on as usual. Washington D.C. can get one inch of snow and school openings are delayed, the trains stop running and the city all but shuts down. Before I even think about stepping out into the sun, I have to slather on goo-gobs of sunscreen and walk around with a gallon of water. I doubt strongly that your average Sudanese is doing the same. So in addition to what your reference point is, it is also about what you may be adapted to.

As I was flying here from Khartoum, the capital city, all I could see from the airplane was sand to the horizon. I knew that if the plane crashed and I survived, my life would have only been prolonged by an hour for I was going to die shortly after that. Upon closer inspection I can see clusters of communities with traces of a road etched in the sand. There is little break in the brown scenery.

After I land, I can tell that I am going to like my new home. On first impressions, Sudanese are very friendly. This dusty back water town has been overrun by foreigners from the United Nations, African Union, and International Non Government Organizations—and I heard even Don Cheadle was in town after being newly awoken to the woes of Africa following his dramatic portrayal in Hotel Rwanda.

The smiles are wide and their clothing is colorful for the women. Men are pretty standard in white flowing robes with a turban twisted and layered on their heads like a charmed snake easing out of its basket.

A good entry point into culture is the market place. El Fasher market does not have the vim and vigor you may see in a West African market too hot for all that hustling, haggling and hounding, though the young boys who want to sell you plastic bags to carry your goods move with you like a shadow.

Today I accompanied the drivers to where they grab a quick lunch. Without a question, the Sudanese throw down on a plate called "foul" which is beans with chunks of tomatoes, onions and green peppers. It is eaten with flat bread. They also ordered a plate of goat meat and another plate of maize gloop and okra squash. I most ignorantly did not bother to learn the names of those plates as they were less enticing.

The restaurant is basically some tree posts covered by mats. It is cool inside as you have to squat to gain access. You sit on four poster stools made of wood and hatch-hair crossings of goat hide for your butt. It was very inviting. The owner,

Sashida, seemed sincerely happy to see me. I could smell incense as soon as I walked in and really wanted to buy some. We went back and forth on how to say it in Arabic and I am still not sure. The next thing I know she is moving towards her pocketbook kept near the stove, and digs in her bag and pulls out a once upon a time Avon bottle. It did not look like it held the secret to beauty. It was a bottle with a gritty substance that wanted to smell sweet, but smelt more like the beans I just got finished eating. Sashida excitedly handed me the bottle and I did not want to disappoint her so I took my pinky and dabbed a little on my wrist. That was 8 hours ago and it is still going strong. It is more of a musk aroma that lingers. It is nice. My assistant pointed out a corner where they sold traditional perfumes. I will pace myself and wait until the end of the week to check it out.

It is challenging to stay hydrated here. I had lathered my neck with Queen Anne's cocoa and shea butter mix and by the morning I thought my skin was going to crack. I am not used to drinking this much to stay healthy. But I am no good to no one sick, so I better try.

It is only my first day and soon the reason why I am here will become more obvious, as I will visit the internally displaced camps that have as many people as a small town. People chased away from their homes—dependant on strangers to keep them alive as all livelihood systems have broken down and probably to them, mankind has broken down.

◆   ◆   ◆

Darfur is a conflict that few really understand. It is doubtfully less complicated than Arab verses African. And probably as simple as people tired of being marginalized, taking up arms to do something about it. But there is an element of manipulation and political exploitation to all conflicts. This is a conflict the U.S. has had its eye on for a very, very long time. Darfur is just the fly in the ointment compared to the gabillions of dollars spent on the north—south war in Sudan that has lasted over two decades. However, Darfur does risk to be that fly that sours the entire stew. A peace accord was signed to effectively end the north—south war. A new government filled with former rebels are positioning to take their pedestal. It is going to look really, really bad to have them another war going on, millions fleeing and thousands killed, while all of this is taking place. So to the Darfur furor, the U.S. has injected nearly one billion dollars over the last two years. I do not pretend to understand all of their reasoning beyond it being the right, humanitarian thing to do. However, I do not doubt there are interests to protect. However, in the meantime, the investment is literally keeping millions of people alive.

But there are times where the investments of the U.S. government put those of us who live overseas in harms way. The world is so much smaller now than it was during the cold war. I move to swat a fly, and my neighbor feels the wind created by my hand. The U.S. has moved forward with such an arrogance and ignorance of the world around us that we have made enemies out of former friends. To be an American overseas, I have to be careful what I say. People are not so happy to see Americans in their country these days, as they were before when I first started traveling. I was in Rwanda when President Clinton came to town. I was not so politically swayed. I had heard a lot about his disarming personality. But I shortly felt myself getting caught up in the fever. I have never seen a president so beloved by Africans, who was not African.

The Man from Hope has needled his way up there in fond memories along with Julius Nyerere and Nelson Mandela. The four hours we waited for him to appear, since 6:00 that morning, was instantly forgotten when he appeared and apologized to the Rwandan people. He disarmed us and swayed us and my blood was flowing red white and blue after his visit. I do not think I will ever know a pride like this again in relation to being an American.

Bush does not command the same respect. My African friends were so engaged with the Bush I term that you though they had a voting card to participate. They knew what the implications were, even 10,000 miles from the White House. Africa was going to be forgotten. Africa compared to Iraq and Afghanistan does not compare. However, to be fair, the U.S. has pumped gabillions of dollars into Sudan. Better that than to have them cozy up to Bin Laden again. The U.S. gets a bad call for having such a small percentage of their GNP go to foreign aid. But that small percentage is so much more money in absolute terms than the Nordic countries who have no standing army and contribute 15-20% of their GNP to foreign aid.

Terrorism made it to the front doors of the White House and the Department of Homeland Security was born. Yes, it changed the way we do business, particularly regarding welcoming those who have nowhere else to live. The number of legal asylum seekers was reduced to 25,000 in 2001 from an average of 50,000-

60,000 in prior years. In 2005, the ceiling has reached 70,000 with the majority being accepted from Africa. The U.S. is the largest grantor of asylum in the world. Canada follows with their ceiling of 5000. Then you can get to a country like Ireland who accepted 150 immigrants to live in their country in 2004.

When I started my international travel, it was glamorous being a diplomat. Now that I am a diplomat, I have to say that it is just dangerous. In certain circumstances I am a target, not for what I said, but for what I represent. But along with the US's arrogance that has brought so much of this upon their squadrons posted around the world on their behalf, it is also the world that has changed, and clearly not for the better. People filming other people cutting off other people's heads. People crashing airplanes into American icons. People blowing up trains and blowing up public opinion; changing the course of political history. The stakes have changed. The downtrodden are no longer meek and they are tired of waiting around to inherit the earth. They too must have their CNN moment. The opportunist will always play their hand in manipulating a situation; fanning the flames of ignorance.

But poverty is real. And poverty is rising up and taking no prisoners. Just today I was talking to a medical doctor. I was taking advantage of his great English to explain to me aspects of Sudanese culture I observed. I was asking about food and why the meal they eat at 11:00 am is called "breakfast". He responded that before the last regime, they used to eat three meals a day, now it is only two. He expected a reaction from me, not knowing that I have spent a lot of time in Burundi where people are eating every other day. To remind him of that would have been rude, so I just nodded with sincerity.

As an American overseas, I cannot minimize my security posture. I just might be the vessel to make a point that is very important to my captors. And perhaps this is why the U.S. is acting like a cowboy on a new frontier. It is a new land, at least to us—but it is still one where the U.S. cannot take its big stick and beat the occupants into submission.

Jennifer Thomas is a writer and humanitarian that hails from New York City.

The Nation

Poor Blacks on the Most Recent Presidential Election and America in General

by Melva Florence

Any number of clichés can be used to define the conditions under which poor blacks are living in America—like "…there is a time and a place for everything." The 40th anniversary of the historic Brown vs. the Board of Education decision was not the time for a self-appointed spokesperson for poor blacks to "…air the dirty laundry" of communities they have never set foot in with the intention of solving the problems. Historically, the US government, the rich, the educated and other blacks themselves have all taken turns verbally attacking the limited achievement of poor blacks. It was the time to reflect on the progress Americans have made in closing the Achievement Gap that has existed since educational needs of public school students have been identified. As the Brown vs. Board of Education case shows the federal government had a hand at creating the impoverished conditions black people are currently living. Accusations of poor blacks "…not taking personal responsibility…" flies in the faces of those people who work hard every day to provide a meager existence for their families. The accusations served to corroborate the ugly stereotypes held by the rest of Americans regarding poor blacks.

Recently the famous comedian Bill Cosby took it upon himself to join the attack on poor blacks in this country with his own hateful, discriminatory, malicious, stereotype—endorsing speeches, whose veracity could be challenged with a simple study of world history. Surprisingly, he readily charged "…poor ignorant" children with destroying the English language and perpetuating the ignorance of their parents. Every documented *civilized* society has expressed issues with the ignorant underclass destroying the language of the land. One of *his* most quoted notable quotes, "A word to the wise ain't necessary, it's the stupid ones that need the advice," negates his recent claim to not be able "…to speak the way these people speak." Whether Bill Cosby's tirades were misguided attempts to galvanize poor blacks, an effort to move back into the public eye without the scandalous paternity drama that drove him from it, ride the wave of publicity for his new movie, or stir up enough controversy to deflect attention from the 40th anniversary reminder that one generation back, it took the Supreme Court to decide separate but equal was unlawful.

Eliminating the cycle of poverty is deeply rooted in obtaining an excellent education, and an excellent education continues to elude poor black children. Schools seem to be less about educating all students and more about identifying, labeling and eliminating the students who can't be taught. Education is the only industry operating in this country that boasts a 67-75% productivity level. Too much of what is wrong in the school system is being blamed on the students. Limited resources prevent schools in the poor neighborhoods from supplementing the education of the children attending them. While president George W. Bush has set about peddling No Child Left Behind legislation all over the country, schools that weren't meeting the requirements of the plan before they became NCLB schools are given two years and no resources to meet the requirements and again the money meant to supplement the changes needed in the schools go to outside companies. It is as if all the plans to solve the problems with education poor children create all new and different problems. Teachers and Administrators across the country are complaining about no parental involvement among poor children's parents. Parents, usually but not always are single mothers with no cars, on welfare who are tenuously holding on to low paying service jobs with extreme attendance requirements in an effort to meet the strict employment requirements of welfare reform.

"Personal responsibility" is the catch phrase for the 21st century, enabling privileged and moneyed individuals, who have always made sure they maintained a place at the table, to sit back and pass judgment on those less fortunate—but less fortunate than whom? President Clinton, with the welfare reform bill signed in 1996, ended the federal entitlement to welfare. Images of the "Welfare Queen" with two buggies of groceries and five kids hanging from each of her appendages danced in their heads at the decision making table as strict work requirement on recipients were coupled with a five year *lifetime* limit for aid. Women, children and the elderly populated the welfare roles in disproportionate numbers and with the strict work requirements on welfare recipients women will be supporting their families for $.76 on the dollar less than men for the same work that men do. Two million people are currently receiving welfare in this country and it is down by 1/3 since the Welfare Reform Bill was enacted, however the poverty level is increasing.

President George W. Bush hails from Texas where the state Constitution prohibits the Legislature from spending more than 1% of the state budget on poor children and by continually delegating social services to nonprofits and giving to nonprofits decreasing allows the government to continue to shuck the responsibility for the conditions of poor blacks. When documented governmental responsibility is attached to the oppression of blacks and undisputable proof from one generation back people are charged with living in the past. Innumerable tax credits are being offered to *developers* to build housing for people making no more than 80% of the median family income in their area. The national median average is about $51,000 annually.

Bill Cosby's comments, regardless of what place they were coming from and the outcome he was expecting, are symptomatic of the apathy repetitiously winding through every aspect of the life of any individual living in poverty. Where is his "School of Comedy," or his "School of Writing," or his secret to success manual that doesn't first exponentially increase his wealth? Clearly his credibility as a comedian is not a cause for concern; Sonny Bono became a Congressman, Arnold Schwarzenegger became governor and Ronald Regan became president. His name has been noticeably absent from any ballot box where any real change can happen. Pointing fingers and looking for someone to blame is as useless as calling out a hypocrite when one happily makes himself know to be one. Another cliché comes to mind on the road to the solution. "Don't judge a man unless you have walked a mile in his shoes." This is one more cliché that if followed would be a big step in solving the problems of poor blacks in this country. Since electing to be black is not an option and very few people would voluntarily be poor, one can only rely on the experience of those that are either or both. It stands to reason that these are the people who need to be at the table plotting the best course of action as to how to attack and eliminate the poverty cycle.

This group, in addition to being attacked for being poor, also bears the distinction of participating the least in civics. "Get out and vote," is repeated over and over again and why these people don't vote is the subject of much debate and recriminations run rampant when poor people complain about their lot in life.

Money, and lots of it, is required to put an individual in a position to effect change in this country. The leadership of this country mimics the paternalistic ideals of plantation owners of the old south. Value and self worth are defined by how much money an individual has, or has the potential to make. In 2001, 22.7% of blacks were considered living below the poverty threshold as established in the mid-1960s compared to 9.9% of whites and the rate of black female-headed households exceeded 35%. Regardless to whether an individual believes this to be true or not, collectively this country values the leadership of white men with money and the realities of growing up and living poor prevent most people from selecting between the lesser of two evils. People with money are interested in keeping it and making more of it and there is nothing wrong with that, neither is looking out for one's own best interest but to impose the what's good for the goose is good for the gander mentality is not the way to solve problems.

The United States is a nation of intolerance, intolerance for the causes that have led to the human condition as it exists today. No federal mandate immediately halting the dependence on welfare without immediately providing jobs paying a livable wage will make a dent in the poverty cycle. Education—fair and equal access to a good education and a productive future is tied to the backs of hardworking black families and their children and dangles elusively just out of reach. Giving a wealthy construction company tax breaks which translates to money in their pocket to build houses doesn't make nearly as much sense as giving the job of building their home to the people who are going to live there. It is easy to get bogged down in finger pointing at Bill Cosby, his ignorant ranting and the reasons behind them; just as a certain satisfaction can be gleaned highlighting his flaws as a businessman, husband and father—while pointing out all the mistakes he has made in his life. The truth of this matter is, everyone makes mistakes, mistakes have consequences and a person should not repeatedly be beaten over the head with their mistakes. While the existence of the cycle of poverty has been postulated upon, studied profusely and the effects of poverty are readily identifiable, poor people have lost the innate value of their human ability to care for themselves and their offspring. It is time to recognize it takes all types of people. Everyone is different and in differences that is our strength and that strength must be represented in our leadership.

Melva Florence is the founder of the LASTRAW (pronounced "last straw"), an organization which seeks to be a representative group enabling low-income citizens, working poor, welfare recipients, and the homeless to be consulted regarding ideas on how to improve their quality of life. Melva lives in the red state of North Carolina, and can be reached by phone at 336-987-9676. Her e-mail address is <u>reapwhatusew_2003@yahoo.com</u>.

A Plan for the Future

by Michael G. McFadden

As a life-long and very liberal/progressive Democrat, I am concerned about our nation's current state of political affairs. The ineffective, in my view, electoral philosophies of those who advocate for policies compatible with my own have led to the ascendancy of politicians with philosophies and "values" anathema to my own—as well as those, I believe, of most Americans.

While there are many important issues, both domestic and foreign, facing our country which require a change in direction, I would like to offer a plan which I believe positively impacts three of our most pressing domestic needs. As I outline the details of my proposal, I will also provide suggestions as to how these programs can be sold to all Americans.

Saving America's retirement security, healthcare, and economic systems

We can reduce the payroll taxes paid by employees from 6.2% to 4% and eliminate the cap. The vast majority of Americans make substantially less than $90,000, so this will result in a huge tax cut for most Americans. This can be sold by using the same language Republicans used regarding the tax cuts they passed over the last couple of years. It will be difficult for them to campaign or vote against this package because it is in simpatico with their language and stated philosophy. I would even suggest using recordings of some of their floor speeches in commercials promoting the plan.

Employees who have an annual income of $90,000 or more will pay a payroll tax rate (for each dollar above $90,000) of 3% up to the first $200,000 of income. Wages in excess of $200,000 will be taxed at a 2% rate for the first $100,000 ($300,000), then 1% for the next $100,000 ($400,000), then 1% for each dollar thereafter. All employees (regardless of income) will receive the same percentage increase, except those employees with incomes of $200,000 or more will receive their increase once every five years, while those with incomes less than $200,000 will receive their increases on an annual basis.

The payroll tax rate paid by employers for their employees who earn wages up to $90,000 will remain at 6.2%, unless the employer provides comprehensive health care for those employees. An employer who provides a "qualifying plan" (eye, dental, and health) for those employees will qualify for a 4% payroll tax rate for those employees. Employers with employees who earn wages in excess $90,000, but less than $200,000, will be subjected to a 3% payroll tax (for each dollar above $90,000). Employers with employees who earn wages of $200,000 or more may see their rate reduced by 1/3 for each additional $100,000 of income, with the rate being 1% for each dollar above $400,000. There will be no payroll tax rate reduction for employer provided health care for employees in this income category ($90,000 or more). The universal appeal of such a plan provides an opportunity to sneak in a little, much needed, social engineering.

The Politics

Opponents of this plan will find themselves campaigning against tax cuts, economic stimulus, employer provided health care (all of which would benefit the vast majority of "Red State Americans"), and shoring up Medicare, while defending benefit cuts and more borrowing under the President's privatization plan, subsidies for pharmaceutical and insurance companies, and Medicare cuts under the President's Medicare Prescription Drug Bill, and 2006 budget.

The Republicans have been complaining that Democrats have not submitted a Social Security (hereinafter referred to as SS) plan. So give them one. Submit both the SS, Estate Tax and Medicare rewrites as a comprehensive plan. The President, in advocating for personal accounts, which are not relevant to the issue of SS solvency, has opened up the debate to one of retirement security, as opposed to solely SS. Thus, all things that factor into providing retirement security for the American people are germane to the debate. Proposing a comprehensive plan (beyond the merits of the plan itself) also provides an opportunity to highlight the shortcomings of the President's Medicare Prescription Drug and Estate Tax Bills in ways that we previously could not. Similar to the untenable arguments our opponents will be forced to make regarding our rewrite of the Prescription Drug Bill, opponents of the Estate Tax rewrite will be forced to argue that the interests of the approximately 30 thousand super rich families that will be subject thereto, should be given priority over the millions of Americans, in all

50 states, who will see their medical benefits cut as a result of the Presidents budget. Governors in all 50 states will support these rewrites because they now face the specter of either raising the eligibility levels, or cutting the benefits they currently provide under Medicaid.

Also the Prescription Drug Bill and the Estate Tax bill rewrites can easily be linked to this issue by demonstrating that, if these bills are rewritten, tax payers will see less of their SS checks eaten up by health care costs, and therefore give them more discretionary spending power. This is also a boost to the economy, and the living standards of our seniors. We often celebrate them as "The Greatest Generation." If we truly believe this, shouldn't we provide them with some recognition of their greatness, particularly where it helps our economy? Our position is much more "patriotic" than that of our opponents, and we should never shrink from saying so. They wouldn't!

Each category of SS beneficiary will receive the same annual % increase, but those with average annual incomes of $200,000 or more will receive their increases once every five years. Under the proposed plan, and similar to the stated rationale for the Bush tax cuts, every American worker will get a tax cut in the same proportion to their contribution to the system. Those with wages above $90,000 will only experience a tax cut up to their first $90,000, and a corresponding tax increase which puts them in the same category as those whose incomes fall below the cap.

This plan will also result in a large tax cut for businesses, particularly small businesses, that have few, if any employees who currently make more then $90,000. Thus, it can't be attacked for being bad for the economy. Again, under the stated theory of the Bush tax cuts, this plan should provide a huge boost to the economy both because these Americans will spend the money when they get it, and this plan may yield the additional benefit of creating significant job growth. It may also make it possible—politically—to raise the minimum wage.

The plan will also provide incentives for companies (think Wal-Mart) to provide health care coverage for their employees, thereby easing our nation's health care crisis. This SS plan—along with rewriting the President's Medicare Prescription Drug Bill to eliminate the subsidies for pharmaceutical and insurance companies, and the prohibition on negotiating prices—will alleviate the need for the proposed Medicare reductions in the President's budget. It also makes sense to, as part of this comprehensive package, raise the cap on the Estate Tax to $3 million, and dedicate all of its' proceeds to Medicare. Since House members are often prohibited from offering alternatives and amendments, we should use the Republicans' insistence that we offer a plan, to offer a plan!

They will no doubt argue that proponents of this plan are simply bowing to liberal interest group pressure. Consider the benefits of conceding the point (rhetorically), and counter with the question that if both political parties are in the pocket of their party funders, which party do Americans believe is looking out for them? The labor unions represent working Americans, the Environmental groups represent Americans concerned with our air, and water. When this is contrasted that who Republican funders are, I think Republicans will quickly abandon that line of attack!

The President and his cohorts have suggested that Democrats are not even aware that a problem exists. This is an opportunity to demonstrate not only that a problem exists in SS, but that we/they realize that the more pressing problem is with Medicare. This turns the tables on Republicans, and will require them to defend the status quo. The media will be all over this, and if we effectively utilize their campaign commercials touting tax cuts, waste, fraud, and economic stimulus, they will be forced to argue with themselves in order to oppose our plan. This will also provide us with an opportunity to highlight all the ethical issues regarding Tom Delay, and how the Medicare Bill was written and passed. The mainstream media will be forced to provide coverage of this.

The amount of the payroll tax rate under my plan has not been scored by an actuary, so the percentages are subject to some modification, but the principle behind it will remain. Democrats need to understand that Republicans will say anything in order to get elected. In fact, the focus of their party seems more directed to getting elected, then governing! That is why, as I am sure you are aware, every piece of legislation they pass (Bankruptcy, Energy, Medicare, etc.), often along partisan lines, lavishes generous benefits on those who fund their campaigns.

The Comprehensive Retirement, Healthcare, and Economic Security Plan Outline:

A. Reduce the overall payroll tax rate from 6.2%, to 4% for all employees earning less than $90,000, and remove the $90,000 cap;

   1. Employees with wages in excess of $90,000 should be taxed at a 3% rate; and

   2. Employees with wages of $200,000 or more may see their rate reduced by 1/3 for each additional $100,000 of income, with the rate being of 1% for each dollar above $400,000.

B. The payroll tax rate for employers will remain 6.2% for all employees who earn $90,000 or less;

   1. The payroll tax rate for all employers will be reduced to 4% if they have or adopt a comprehensive health care benefit for their employees earning $90,000 or less; and

   2. Employers with employees who earn wages in excess of $90,000 should be taxed at a 3% rate; and

   3. Employers with employees who earn wages of $200,000 or more may see their rate reduced by 1/3 for each additional $100,000 of income, with the rate being 1% for each dollar above $400,000.

C. Employers with employees with annual incomes in excess of $90,000 should be given a 1-% tax credit for providing "comprehensive" health care for their employees;

D. Retirees who had and average annual income of $200,000 or more will receive the same cost of living increases as all other retirees (based on prices) with annual average incomes of less then $200,000, except that they will receive these increases every five years;

E. The President's Medicare Prescription Drug Bill should be rewritten (as part of this comprehensive plan) to provide for the ability to negotiate lower drug prices, and remove all subsidies and tax breaks. The savings will be dedicated to Medicare;

F.   The Estate Tax repeal should be rewritten to raise the cap to $3 million and have its proceeds dedicated to Medicare.

You cannot win an election against folk who are willing to say anything, if you constrain yourself to behaving in a manner consistent with the majesty of the office you seek. Politics is an honorable profession, but getting elected has become like making sausage! In an atmosphere awash in appeals to patriotism, they were nonetheless willing and able to savage Max Cleland! These folks have no shame, and their shameless appeals win elections.

The underlying rationale for this bold and comprehensive plan is to rescue our health care, and retirement security programs, while providing tax relief for the vast majority of Americans, and economic stimulus for our economy. When elected representatives and political operatives do the network and cable talk show circuit, they should be very disciplined in their language, and never fail to promote this as a bold, comprehensive, and patriotic plan to rescue all Americans from their pending health care and retirement security crisis.

An Observation on "The Cult of POTUS"

by Elgin D. Lewis, Jr.

Many of us in "Blue States," and those of us in "Red States" who have a "Blue State of Mind," are perplexed by the intense loyalty generated among supporters of George W. Bush. Their passion for him is so single-minded that it seems alien to us. Perhaps that is because "Blue Staters" are not of a single mind.

Many of us are not even Democrats. Some of us are self-described as 'liberal,' and some, as 'moderate.' A growing number answer to the name of 'true' conservatives. Others, still, prefer the term, 'libertarian.' We are like fans of a struggling baseball team who think that the manager should be fired. Some of us want him gone because he bunts too much, but the rest of us might want him fired because he doesn't bunt enough. We don't agree unanimously on anything, except that the current regime needs to be changed.

Bush supporters don't suffer ambiguity. They believe in Bush, they trust in Bush, and they feel safe with Bush. No amount of contradictory evidence, documentation, or proof can change their minds. However, in keeping their faith, they have to overlook a number of glaring inconsistencies, such as the following:

When George W. Bush was governor, the state of Texas fought legal battles to preserve the right to execute teenagers, the mentally retarded, and murder defendants with sleeping, drug-addicted lawyers. Later, Bush's state budgets delayed, and then tried to restrict, health services for poor children, when the state already led the nation in the numbers of children who had inadequate medical coverage. Right now, as President, Bush wages war against a nation which had never threatened, and could never have threatened, the United States, even if it had wanted to.

Ignoring all that, a few weeks ago George W. Bush proudly proclaimed his leadership role in helping America build a new "culture of life." Bush supporters hardly batted an eyelash at the stark irony. 'Blue Staters' couldn't have missed it. This Observer finds it hard to associate George W. Bush with a "culture of life." On the other hand, I find it much easier to make a case that Bush has succeeded in creating a cult...that is, the "Cult of POTUS."

What is a "Cult?"

A GROUP OF PEOPLE WHO:
Give total and unquestioning loyalty to a leader as a living deity or prophet.
Use deception and manipulation to recruit and keep members.

HAS A LEADER (OR LEADERS) WHO:
Is charismatic.
Holds a uniquely exalted position.
Claims an exclusive relationship with God, truth, happiness, etc.

THE GROUP EXPECTS:
Complete and total loyalty and obedience to the leader.
Complete and literal acceptance of the leader's teachings.
Unquestioning devotion to the group and its leader.

CULTS ARE:
Unethical in their practices.
Designed to advance the goal of the group's leader, often to the detriment of its members.
Dangerous because they separate people from their families, friends and other support networks. In this way, cults foster in their members feelings of complete dependency and sometimes isolation from outside influences
—From The Cult Hotline and Clinic, New York City, New York: http://www.cultclinic.org

George W. Bush has long proclaimed a deep, "special" relationship with God. As early as 1999, Bush told religious leaders that he believed that "God wants me to be president." Two years ago, he told the Palestinian Prime Minister that God told him to attack Al-Qaeda, and then directed him to attack Iraq. As recently as the last political campaign, Bush was reported to have said, "I trust God speaks through me."

Leaving aside how alarming those statements are, considering the position that Bush occupies, they illustrate how well his political team capitalizes on his religious message. They exploit the depth of Bush's personal faith, in order to sustain the depth of his political power, among his core supporters. True Believers take these statements quite literally. When Bush is open about being a 'God-fearing man,' his 'witness' earns him an unshakeable reputation for 'moral strength,' 'sincerity,' and 'honesty.'

To get the rest of us 'with the program,' however, the Bush team employs a different tactic. They doctor the information that we receive. And, the methods they use to do so are usually far removed from morality, sincerity, or honesty. In just the last few weeks, we've learned that:

The White House produces and packages fictitious 'news' reports, created to air during local news broadcasts. The packages are disguised as 'factually objective,' when, in fact, they are designed to promote the administration's side of a political argument;

Bush Administration Cabinet officials have paid hundreds of thousands of taxpayers' dollars, under the table, to friendly news 'columnists.' In return, those columnists have offered their 'independent' opinions in favor of the administration's political agenda on education, welfare, and marriage; and,

A 'reporter,' appearing prominently at White House press conferences, regularly asked nationally televised 'questions' of the President and his Press Secretary which were unmistakably slanted in the administration's favor. The news 'agency' he worked for turned out to be a front, funded by one of Bush's longtime contributors. The 'reporter,' himself, was a phony; he received WH press passes from the Press Secretary's office, daily,...and, even in this era of heightened national security concern, he received them under a fictitious name.

When these deceptions were exposed publicly, the Bush team barely shrugged their shoulders. They delivered facile, off-handed excuses: "Well, those 'information' packages have been done before...Okay, okay, we won't pay columnists to do that anymore...Yes, sure, we'll look into how that guy got past us." So far, they have not been called upon to address the pattern of their dishonesty. Meanwhile, they continue to hide the origin and the quality of the information that we receive. They continue to deceive us about the purposes for which we are receiving it.

Most troubling about this dishonesty is how easily we have come to accept it. Many Americans—'cult members,' if you will—choose to give up their right to be informed truthfully about their own government. They trust, completely, in George W. Bush. They trust, faithfully, that such a "strong moral leader" is divinely guided to take us where the country needs to go. And, they trust, simply, that whatever the Administration does, it is in our own 'best interests.'

How did Americans reach this point? "9-11 Changed Everything"

The news headlines for September 10, 2001, were nothing out of the ordinary. Time Magazine's issue was typical. It carried profile features on the 'new' Administration's key figures; on domestic and international politics; on kids and hyperactivity drugs; and, on a 'distressing' Little League baseball scandal.

Life, in other words, rolled on.

On the morning of September 11, all that changed abruptly, tragically...and, seemingly, inexplicably. By Tuesday afternoon, Americans' concerns could be summed up in three simple questions:

Are you all right? Who could have done this to us? Why do they hate us?

Overnight, millions became ripe for 'cult' recruitment, as Dr. Robert J. Lifton demonstrated in his 8 Criteria for Thought Reform (http://www.ex-cult.org/General/lifton-criteria):

Environmental Control—The purposeful limitation of all forms of communication with the outside world.

Mystical Manipulation—Extensive personal manipulation is used to provoke specific patterns of behavior and emotion in such a way that they will appear to have arisen spontaneously.

The Demand for Purity—The world is sharply divided between pure and impure with the group in the role of ultimate judge. Normal urges and tendencies become sins, and shame is used to control.

Confession—Carried beyond its ordinary expressions to the point of becoming a cult itself. This enhances the group's hold upon the person and their guilt; is an act of symbolic self-surrender; is a means of maintaining a tone of total exposure; and makes it impossible to attain a reasonable balance between worth and humility.

The aura of *Sacred Silence*—Prohibiting any questioning of the basic dogma, the cult's laws, regulations and rules are absolute and must be followed.

Loading the language—Characterized by the thought-terminating cliché. The most complex of problems are compressed into brief, definitive sounding phrases, easily memorized and expressed.

Doctrine Over Persons—The value of an individual member is insignificant compared to the value of the group.

Dispensing of Existence—The cult environment draws a sharp line between those whose right to existence can be reorganized and those who possess no such right. The religious cult draws a sharp line between not only those who will or will not be saved but other individuals and groups who are not acceptable.

America had been attacked. We were singled out for attack, precisely because we were Americans. The world gave us their sympathy and promised their support, but we felt isolated. We were, in fact, isolated. Commercial public transportation was suspended for days, for security reasons. For several hours, phone lines and internet service was down, all over the country. We stayed connected through network and cable news television.

We spent hours gazing at somber, flag-pin wearing news anchors. We spent days immersed in grief, rage, and, especially, fear. How can we ever feel 'safe' again?

Over the next several weeks, it became clear that our President had the answers. His messages were mixed, but they were easy to understand.

We were attacked, because they hate our freedoms, and they think we are weak. But, we value our freedom of speech; it's what makes us American, and what helps keep us strong. Just to be safe, however, we'll need the authorities to have access to your library records and bookstore purchases. We have to stop the terrorists from using public information to do us more harm. Trust us, though, you innocent Americans will have nothing to fear.

We shouldn't listen to any communications critical of American policy regarding our new mission. They only give aid and comfort to our enemies. Indeed, some of them may contain coded messages for the terrorists, and help them to coordinate their activities against us1. We won't make it easy for the terrorists to change our way of life.

And, though we are a peaceful and friendly people, our new philosophy will be to 'get' our enemies, before they can 'get' us. Also, we shall define our enemies more carefully. Anybody who is not 100% 'with' us, in all that we have to do, will be considered to be 'with' the enemy terrorists. There are no other options.

That goes for Americans, too.

We value our freedom to disagree. It is the very reason that the evildoers attacked us. But, now is a time to be resolute, and not a time for questions. Questions make us appear weak. And, weakness invites the evil ones to attack again. Dissent is bad. It is naïve, at best, and it is disloyal, at worst. It places all of us at greater risk, and makes us all less secure. True Patriots understand that, now, America must speak with one voice.

Our enemies attacked us to create fear in the hearts of a good, God-fearing people. We won't give in to it. We'll defeat the fear with yards of plastic sheeting, and with rolls of duct tape. We shall be careful not to open 'strange' mail, from places we've never been, or from people we don't know. We must keep canned foods and bottled water on hand, enough to last several days, just in case. And, we shall be aware of the Homeland Security Color Code, 24 hours a day, and seven days a week.

We shall defeat the terrorists by yielding, voluntarily, some of the very things for which we were attacked. We shall defend our way of life by making alterations in the way we live. We shall feel and be more secure, collectively, by feeling and acting less secure, individually. Most importantly, we shall defeat our fear by being prepared…to be very afraid.

If, as Americans, we stand resolute, then we all shall be made safer. Patriotic Americans had no choice but to unite behind the strong leadership of George W. Bush. Fearful Americans dared not risk anything else. They dared not think anything else. And, so, they, too, lined up quietly, and saluted.

Breaking the Grip?

There is evidence that the grip of the 'cult of POTUS' may be weakening.

Eighteen months after America began 'standing resolute,' and 'backing the President 110%,' we initiated a pre-emptive war of self-defense against Iraq. Two years of military occupation, a Senate Intelligence Committee investigation, and a special, bipartisan Presidential commission all have determined that Iraq had no weapons of mass destruction at the time of our invasion. Nor, it turns out, could they have produced any.

Now, however, two years after our mission has been 'accomplished,' the streets of Baghdad are not littered with the rose petals thrown by a grateful people for their American liberators. Instead they are littered with car bombs, broken buildings, and human bodies. As of this writing, over 1800 American soldiers have been killed; ten thousand maimed or seriously injured; and, tens of thousands of Iraqis have been killed or injured. Anti-American terrorist recruitment is estimated to be at an all time high1. Pro-American feeling around the globe is at an all-time low.

As a result, the number of Americans who believe that Bush 'misled' us into the Iraq war is rising steadily. Those who think the Iraq war was a 'mistake' is at the highest response levels ever recorded. And, the number of those who have come to feel that the war 'wasn't worth it' is now the majority of Americans polled. Meantime, domestically, national unemployment has risen over a full percentage point. Inflation has reawakened. Historic national budget surpluses have been turned into historic national budget deficits, in part because of the invasion. And, there seems to be no end in sight.

George W. Bush's overall job rating among the American electorate is now below 45% approval. Today, a majority of us say that we believe the country is heading in the 'wrong direction' under his leadership. Yet, Bush's core political base…the 'cult members'…remain loyal, as ever. Millions of them, to this day, are convinced that we did find WMD in Iraq, which only confirms the necessity of our actions. Despite surging terrorist recruitment, they feel safer because of POTUS' conduct of the 'war on terror.' After all, there hasn't been another 9-11 since he declared his war on terror, has there?

They don't hold Bush accountable for any of the economic failures. The deficits, unemployment, the recession…that was mostly due to the terrorists. The rest of it was Bill Clinton's fault. Besides which, nothing else matters, unless America is safe.

To his faithful supporters, George W. Bush is still an honest, God-fearing man of moral strength and integrity. Following his leadership still makes them feel safe. Questioning his leadership is not just unpatriotic; even worse, it is sacrilegious.

Scant months ago, George W. Bush stood for election. Powered by the unflagging zeal of his True Believers, he won. There is evidence that the grip of "the Cult of POTUS" may be weakening, yes,…but, there is proof that it is not weakening fast enough.

How can we hasten the process?

Your first impulse is to tell them they are stupid. Your first impulse is probably wrong.

The two basic principles of psychological coercion are:
If you can make a person BEHAVE the way you want, you can make that person BELIEVE the way you want.
Sudden, drastic changes in environment lead to heightened suggestibility and to drastic changes in attitudes and beliefs.

Remember the assault is on your emotions, not on your intellect.

"The 'Cult of POTUS' encompasses about half of our society, with tens of millions of members spread across the country. The collective literature on the topic of cults doesn't address organizations on that kind of scale. And, cases of former members leaving small cults in small numbers show that even that can be a difficult thing to accomplish.

Still, that is where we are going to have to start.

At times, it is easy to doubt that there is any common reality to work from when talking with a Bush supporter. First, one might attempt debate and persuasion, but often that seems fruitless. The 'cult member' doesn't appear to be listening to anything you say. He probably *isn't*.

Then, it becomes easy to refer to the 'cult member's' views as "simple-minded," or "sheep-like," out of frustration. But that does not have much positive effect, either. It only hardens his resolve, and drives him deeper into his faith. The literature suggests a different approach, one of engagement.

Keep the lines of communication open, as much as possible. Try not to belittle the 'cult's' philosophy, even when it seems that much of their argument revolves around belittling other points of view, and the people who express them. Remember that, for the last 4 years, that is what they've been taught.

Don't let their arguments get personal, and don't take them personally. Instead, try to understand how they got there, from here. Ask, "Why do you believe this?" instead of shouting, "How can you BELIEVE this?!"

Research the 'cult,' itself, more closely. We should know more about who promotes their philosophy, and where they come from. For example, many of us have heard of the Project for a New American Century. Much of the brainpower of the current Administration originates from that organization. Their foreign policy publications and lectures in the 1990's were blueprints for the kind of policies they are enacting upon the world today.

Most 'ordinary' Bush supporters adhere to the agenda of the PNAC. But, few of them know even what the PNAC is.

WE should. We need to know all there is to know about PNAC, and their sister organizations. They are the ones who lead our nation in these 'interesting' times. Then, we must document as much as we can. Record, however formally or informally, the attitudes and expressions of our 'cult members.' We should note, for ourselves, anything that associates with 'cult of POTUS' philosophy, and how it shapes our 'cult members' actions. Note any changes, oddities, or peculiarities in their avowed political philosophy, and in their 'worldly,' day-to-day actions. Be prepared to point out the internal inconsistencies and contradictions of the 'cult' philosophy, when the opportunities present themselves. We never know which cracks in the wall we can develop, through which a little light might shine.

Finally, 'non-cult' members need to network among ourselves. The exchange of information gives us access to broader experiences. We can learn, from each other, what works and what doesn't.

For the next three years, we are stuck with the POTUS that we have now. That doesn't mean that we are stuck with the 'cult' philosophy, for that long. Any system of thought or beliefs, which depends so heavily on fear and deceit to advance its goals, is doomed to crumble under its own weight.

Eventually.

We can begin to chip away at it, where we must, and blow it up, where we can. Our job is to be active,…but also, our job is to be patient. As maddening as that might seem, this Observer holds to an idea that was once expressed to him, this way:

"They can 'get away with it' indefinitely. But, they can not 'get away with it' infinitely."

Elgin D. Lewis, Jr. has taught public school in Houston for several years, works with the elderly, and is a writer and political analyst. He resides in the red state of Texas.

The Hypocrisy of It All!

by James E. Sykes, Jr.

America: Land of the Free and home of the brave. All things considered, I guess it's somewhat free and maybe even brave in spots. Certainly where you stand on this point depends on where you are situated within the fabric of America. Generally speaking, I am as patriotic as the next American. I too love this country for it is my home. However, I don't engage in blind love within my personal relationships nor will I do so with respect to my country.

The truth is that if you live in America and are not able to trade using the advantages of white skin privilege, or if you happen to be a member of an economically challenged group (an American euphemism for being poor, uneducated or mis-educated), then you probably have failed to see much of the freedom and bravery. In fact, you probably thought that "Land of the free and home of the brave" were just more fancy platitudes from the nationalist propaganda machine. It probably never troubled you because for those who find themselves somewhat disenfranchised, they never believed they were substantive assertions.

Let's look at this assertion and some others. Let's take for instance "We hold these truths to be self-evident that all men are created equal and that they are endowed by their creator with certain inalienable rights. That among these are life, liberty and the pursuit of happiness." The patriot that lives inside me loves the sentiment expressed here. But the African-American man who had routinely faced overt discrimination in the education system, the job market, the legal system and in my dealings in all the major areas of life that comprise a thriving society, has a difficult time squaring the platitudes with my reality. In fact, many Americans seem to have missed what assuredly must have been the fine print in the declaration. I have often heard it said that the bold print giveth and the fine print taketh away. I read that assertion and I can't help but think that perhaps the Native American population, African-American population and perhaps the collective of others who belong to marginalized groups must not have read the fine print contained in the declaration. Didn't the fourteenth amendment to the constitution define who was to be considered an American? In fact, it did articulate who was to be considered an American, as audacious as that might seem to those who were here in this land long before it was called America. And forgive me, but weren't those folks already in pursuit of better lives and various liberties? Remind me again, who was it that determined their humanity had no worth?

Who was it that decided that African-Americans had no rights which the white man was obligated to respect? Wasn't it the courts of this land that issued the Dred Scott decision? White supremacist doctrine and racist mores were elevated from being local racist practices to being woven into the very fabric of the country as they were written into legislation and became the law of the land. These laws effectively legalized the rape, kidnapping and never-ending brutality of African-Americans and those who would assist them in their struggle to attain freedom or life, liberty and the pursuit of happiness as it has been described.

It was centuries of dehumanizing, torturous and inhumane treatment of these Americans, code named Slavery, which was the foundation of the economic development of the entire young nation. This nation that we patriotic Americans proudly proclaim to be the richest most powerful nation on earth is whatever it is because of the hundreds of years of free labor that it stole through the generations of slavery. This nation owes its very existence to those African-Americans. Its wealth was amassed on their backs in their blood.

I find it interesting that the current conservative movement across the country espouses pulling ones' self up by their bootstraps. Even more audacious than that is the suggestion those who are marginalized and disenfranchised have only themselves and their lack of discipline to blame. I hear the overt assertion as well as the innuendo that they don't possess the same integrity and work ethic as the majority group. To those people who are foolish enough to assert publicly such ridiculous ideology today I would respond by saying thank God these groups had different ethics. Had they not, I wonder how many other groups would have shared the same tragic story.

How is it that certain people in the leadership of this country can stand and talk for hours about the origins of this country as an outgrowth of religious and political intolerance? How is it that they have audacity to speak of forming a place that those leaving intolerance could come and live and work and prosper?

And how is it that they always manage to leave out the part where they stole four hundred years of free labor and economic growth from a peaceful people who too wanted a better way of life? Why doesn't their conversation include the millions of people who they killed because they wouldn't submit to the murderous indignity and inhumane realities of slavery?

I am consistently amazed at the honor bestowed upon many of the so-called founding leaders of this country while always managing to conveniently leave out the part about how they were serial rapists, misogynists and murderers. Now their modern-day counterparts want to preach about Christian conservatism and family values. Even at this very moment, the President of the United States of America is requesting that we spend nearly $200 Billion dollars in Iraq to rebuild the schools, roads, mosques and other infrastructure items that we are continuing to bomb and destroy even as we send the money. But wait, there's more. While the President asks for the $200 Billion for Iraq, he's also committing our country to spend $300 Billion for relief for the tsunami victims. Here's the punch line: While he's committing us to this $500 Billion dollar obligation, he's also cutting out money for prescription drug plans, senior care, head start and early childhood education. He's cutting out money for substance abuse programs and job training programs. He's cutting out money for higher education. All right here in the land of the free and home of the brave.

Is Mr. Bush aware that unemployment is at staggering levels for various groups of Americans? Does Mr. Bush realize that the public school systems in America are suffering just like the tsunami victims? Can our President be so out of touch with what's going on here at home as to not know that economic hardships are creating great strains on the American family and in many instances are contributing to its break up? Someone should tell our President that though we haven't had an excess of water, despite there not having been a great flood among us, many Americans feel as though they too have been hit by a tsunami. And even as they watch the world news with great compassion, they wonder where their relief will come from.

My experience here in the land of the free and the home of the brave is that our politicians are prodigious purveyors of platitudes. They speak voluminously about our responsibility to lead in the world community. As I understand their rhetoric, our nation has garnered this responsibility in part because of our perceived (declared) status as the "richest most powerful nation in the world." With the steadily declining economy and steadily rising national debt and trade deficit, I wonder how this particular assertion squares with the reality of our nation. In this nation with the ever widening gap between the have and have-nots, how do our leaders measure wealth? Is it money, possessions or perhaps military might that makes us wealthy? Is it the respect we command/demand around the globe? Mr. Bush, how do you measure wealth? What is it that you value?

I value a nation that respects all of her people as well as the people of the world. I am an American and a patriot. I love my country even as I find myself critical of her behavior. I am an American parent. And if I noticed my children were acting inappropriately or in an ill advised or improper manner, I would challenge them on it. I would honor my obligation to point out the error of their ways and to correct their behavior when necessary. I would be irresponsible if I failed to do so. But for some reason this nation that touts its responsibility to lead the world community seems to repeatedly fall short of accepting its responsibilities to many of its own citizens. In addition, the leadership often tries to demonize or vilify any person who holds a viewpoint which is critical of its actions. Like responsible parents a responsible citizenry has a duty to question, comment on and correct ill-advised behavior when they see it.

That being said, I would ask if we are the richest most powerful nation in the world, then why are our children lagging behind in educational skills as compared to the children of Europe and Asia? If this is in fact the case, then why it is that while her warriors are fighting on foreign soil their families are often left to fall into disarray? Why are their loved ones losing their homes? Why aren't their jobs waiting for them when they return? Why are their medical claims being denied en masse? I wonder if our President even understands how incongruent his assertions and his actions are.

If America is truly the home of the brave, then why can't her leaders, the self proclaimed owners of personal responsibility, seem to face up to the horrific tragedies this country has visited upon many of its own people? It appears that only irrefutable historical evidence and a slight twinge of shame moves them to even acknowledge the heinous acts of their past. Even while they call for sanctions against various leaders and nations around the world for crimes against humanity, even while they engage in regime change allegedly for the liberation of people, they refuse to hold themselves accountable for the actions of their own government. In fact, they continue to try and suggest to the victims of their own atrocities that it's all in the past. One shouldn't continue to dwell on those matters. The truth is that remnants of those atrocities are alive and well and are woven into the very fabric of our nation. They are not in the past; they remain here in the present. And if we continue to passively accept the glaring void of true leadership, character and integrity then they will be there in the future as well.

If this is the land of the brave, then when will America summon the courage to officially apologize to the victims of the single most horrific, dehumanizing and shameful crime against humanity to have ever taken place? America was able to summon the courage to apologize to Japanese Americans for their shameful internment during World War II. America has been able to find the courage to constantly apologize to Jewish Americans for the crimes committed against them throughout their history here and abroad. They even built monuments to memorialize and pay tribute to those who survived those tragedies. America has made some half-hearted apologies to Native Americans for the heinous crimes committed against them—although they haven't returned any of what they took!

When will America issue an official and sincere apology for the crimes against Africans, African-Americans and humanity that it committed while hypocritically talking about their obligation to spread democracy and freedom around the world? America is a large glass house. President Bush and the leadership of our great country need to focus more on getting their own house in order before traveling the globe, spending our children's futures on rebuilding countries that their foreign policy and bombs destroyed. They should muster the courage to own up to the Federal institution that was slavery in America before they concern themselves with ethnic cleansing in Bosnia. They should honor their obligations here at home ensuring fair elections and inclusion here before trying to establish a voting democracy in Iraq. They should commit themselves to rebuilding the broken public school systems, legal and healthcare systems in America before committing to rebuilding Sri Lanka and other regions of the globe.

Mr. Bush and this government should know that slavery was a tsunami that hit African-Americans in this country. What resources will he commit to rectifying that egregious wrongdoing? Even as we speak about being the land of free and the home of the brave, even as we purport to support equality of opportunity for all Americans, we still see people being locked away and warehoused without due process. Even as we purport to be about tolerance, many Americans driving the inter-states of this nation don't feel safe because of racial profiling by those who are sworn to protect them. There is no crime in being of African descent or in belonging to a group that has been marginalized.

This country and its leaders have espoused the virtues of liberty and justice for all for centuries. Yet as a nation we are still asking the same questions asked by Frederick Douglass, Booker T. Washington, Dr. Martin Luther King, Jr. and W.E.B. DuBois—"When will America live up to the true meaning of its creed?" I would ask "what profiteth a man if he gains the world and loses his soul?"—and I believe Mr. Bush should ask himself that same question. Now is the time for personal responsibility. If our President and our nation can't stand up and do the right things, then the real tsunami is yet to come. When you listen to the rhetoric of our national leadership and when you scrutinize closely the actions which follow, one can't help but to think…the hypocrisy of it all!

James E. Sykes, Jr. is the author of "Our Voices: Romance, Religion & Rage." He lives with his wife and kids in the red state of Colorado.

The War

Questions

by Eric Stumacher

In this time of continuing horror in Iraq and elsewhere in the world, I invite you to visit, or revisit, these questions:

1. If we want tomorrow to be different from today, what are we willing to do differently today from what we did yesterday?

2. If we say we want peace, what are we willing to change to achieve it?

3. Does it help us to know that our enemy is a human being like us, and not a demon?

4. What would we do if a Native American were to knock on our door and say to us that our land used to be his land, and that our house used to be his house?

5. How would we find motivation in our life if we were not at war?

6. Can we find the courage to lead the way by forgiving first?

7. What kinds of unifying forces can we identify in our lives which can inspire us to live in cooperation with our enemy?

8. What is a "just" war?

9. What would happen if control of Holy Sites around the world were shared?

10. What does it mean about our humanity and our worth as human beings if we are either chosen or not chosen by God?

11. Can we learn to be so proud of our heritages that we can celebrate differences without being threatened by them?

12. If we can play beautiful music together with our enemy, what does that show us?

13. If we were to need an organ transplant, would an Israeli organ, or an Arab organ, or an African organ, or an Asian organ, or a European organ, work equally well?

14. Why has every war in history been justified on both sides by invoking God's will?

15. Are we afraid of peace?

16. If not now, when?

Eric Stumacher is the Pianist for the Apple Hill Chamber Players, and the Executive and Artistic Director, Apple Hill Center for Chamber Music and Playing for Peace. He resides in the blue state of New Hampshire.

Parenthood and War

by Walik Edwards

Voting for who I want to be my president used to be an easy thing. Usually it comes down to party, but if my Dem isn't exactly convincing me that his way is going to make a whole lot of sense for four years, I really have to sit in my special place and contemplate whether I can get the nerve to punch a hole in a GOP slot.

I was driving on a different road in 2004 because I became a father at the half-time mark of the year, and suddenly my voting was sensitized by parenthood.

As an avid news follower, there were too many stories on a daily basis with parents talking about the loss of their young son or daughter in a war I felt could have been avoided—more so when the particulars of the initial reasoning proved to be errant at best.

While Prince continues to search for his talent in Minneapolis, he did manage to put a great song on his underrated 1991 album "Diamonds and Pearls" called "Money Don't Matter 2Night." In that song, there is a line that sticks on you like glue that says:

> "Hey now, maybe we can find a good reason
> 2 send a child off 2 war.
> So what if we're controllin' all the oil,
> Is it worth a child dying 4? (is it worth it?)
> If long life is what we all live 4
> Then long life will come 2 pass.
> Anything is better than the picture of the child
> In a cloud of gas
> And u think u got it bad."

The influence there was probably the first Gulf War, but I'm not talking just my child or an American child—but any child. Children are caught in the crossfire of battle on a regular basis, and that's just what the fates have rung up as a natural occurrence here on Mother Earth.

When the numbers of warriors begin to wane, we'll need more flesh and blood to wear their shoes and walk in their footsteps.

It has unnerved me that there may very well be a mandatory military draft soon, and a tenet that is held in Rosetta stone for the next 18 years or so. It's naïve to think that an invasion to Iraq would go the duration of a network sit-com. There were so many unplanned nuances happening there that it is not out of my personal belief system that the Los Angeles Clippers could be NBA champions by the time this situation is resolved.

There are enough younger people who agreed with the invasion into Iraq, and because there are other countries who match the same parameters as candidates for the same treatment, my son, and the sons of other friends of mine could be fighting off those clouds of gas Prince is shaking his head in disdain about.

And venturing back to solidify a point I started with in my prior paragraph, there are younger people in complete agreement with the war in Iraq and a hand-ful of those young people are blessed with charisma, and a fraction of those may entertain running for President one day.

It's not in my usual modus operandi to plan too far ahead, but when you see your baby struggling to sit up on his own today, and knowing he will conquer that ability along with many others in his history of infancy-to-adulthood, and be able enough to have a rifle and battle equipment strapped to his back because a mandate says he has to fight for his country, nothing matters more than stopping something like that before it gets a chance to get started.

The rumors were at DefCon 15 that if there were more red-state electoral votes by the end of Election Day, there would probably be more countries to man-up against, and the flesh and blood representation had to grow exponen-tially because we're learning that the rest of the world is ready to put up their dukes against us, and go to the grave if they have to.

These are probably things that should have come to mind a long time ago. It's human nature to contain a little equilibrium when the face of another's loved one is flashed on a screen graced by rank, date of birth and death, but what if?

We don't plan parenthood for a 23-year run. I want to be old enough to be a parent of a college graduate, and a grandparent, but the fear is that a draft is on the horizon, and there's nothing that can be done to stop it. The red-state people have the controls at the moment, and a parent's prayer shifts to hoping to end bloodshed, and hoping my child never has to encounter anything more than an "ouchie" on his knee or somewhere.

We all come from different alleyways to our gods, and we all believe that they are all accepting of what we put out there regardless. For the most part, everyone's god is a forgiving god. A god needs to be because sometimes we have to shake the tree a little to make our beliefs come to fruition.

As long as our gods are forgiving gods, there is no true wrong or right, or wrongs that can be forgiven without consequence, as long as the reasoning rests well within our own heart. War is something that needs to happen according to some of those whose god condemns kilter, slight or otherwise, off free speech, but believes to clean up the world may require the elimination of a few unfavorable types.

It's the Great Flood all over again, just with a lot more bloodshed and a greater length than just 40 days.

I believed that a try at diplomacy would take place if the election went the way I hoped. It's not in this administration to negotiate, but to rush heavy into dispute with caustic words first, then using the children of frightened mothers second.

In all, it's brought me to a point to overly saturate myself with my son. I know I have at least 18 good years with him, and when I punched my blue-state influenced ticket, I was just hoping to be guaranteed a little more than that.

Walik Edwards has transitioned from writing his interoffice "CubeFour Sports" e-mail daily to being one of the movers and shakers at Sportsology.net. An unabashed Yankee fan, Walik lives with his wife and son in the blue state of California. Visit him online at cubefoursports.com.

Letter from the Front Line

by John Smith

This was a letter I wrote while relaxing (well, trying to relax) at least a couple of hours before a mission. I was describing to loved-ones the many aspects of the war. I am blessed to have been able to look back at this letter and say I made it through many situations that most wouldn't want to imagine. In this letter, I try to stress the point of being thankful for what we have and no matter how the odds may seem against us, pray for change and God will make a way.

Dear loved-one,

I sit supine against a rock pretending the zephyr which animated sand on my cheeks was my ceiling fan at home, and not another black hawk chopper passing, but the realization has long since sunk in.

It's close to the fourth of July (about five days, to be exact) but these fireworks aren't what I long for. In a sense, these explosions and gunfire are in some uncanny way characteristics of humanity that should never be over looked, but too often are. The epitome of those who have and those who have not.

A young black male, twenty years old in the midst of a substance which, at one point in time, was only known to me through television (news). Nothing on TV could have truly prepared me for the first time I saw a woman and child begging soldiers, begging me, for food—for water. This deformed the reality I believed deep down inside, that their lives weren't as bad as news depicted. There is no way I can truly write the emotions that overcome me when looking into a hungry child's eyes. All I can say is, it changes you.

I guess habitual acts of negligence will eventually numb empathy. That's the only way I can begin to imagine those here in Iraq who has been able to look into each other's eyes with indifference. I can't help but think the core of this war, of any war, is greed. I don't want to get into politics too much, but this war is wrong, making me question my involvement in it. But I am a soldier, so I follow orders. I am human first and feelings like this aren't easy to abide with.

If I could go back and retrieve one long lost wish of any of the soldiers preceding me, it would undoubtedly be for war to be non existent. But the surreal situation I am placed in has shown me that wishes too often become long lost dreams that reflect how cruel reality can actually be. So I continue to pray, each and every day because I know that is my most powerful weapon. Well, I have to get ready to go on a mission now, so I will try to write to you again later.

Love always,

John

John Smith—not his real name—is in the Army Reserves. He is home now.

The 4-1-1 on Fahrenheit 911

by Marion Boykin

It was a very small vest-pocket type theater. I had noticed it a few times on my way home on the bus. Perhaps it had been one of those old porn theaters back in the day, as it looked terribly out of place in a Northern New Jersey town not big enough to have enough people to fill it. Though it usually presented foreign films, on this day I passed it I noticed that it was playing the Michael Moore documentary, "Fahrenheit 911."

I had wanted to see this movie for some time and as we were quickly approaching Election Day in November, I thought I'd sneak off and catch it one day soon. With the star of the movie being George Bush, perhaps it might be funny, in a serious sort of way. Perhaps a dark comedy or at least something I could learn from. Though I already had a good understanding of how things were being done regarding this administration, especially as it pertained to why we were there in Iraq in the first place. Weapons of mass destruction, and the quickly uncovered fact that we found none, put me at ill at ease to say the least. Mix in our kids going off to a war and dying under a wrong interpretation of why they thought they were there and you end up in a different kind of Oz, not with lions and tigers and bears, but with lies and deceit and death, oh my!

I happened to be off one day and at home with my son. A day off from school is always an appreciated thing, from elementary to college. I thought I'd offer a movie to my boy, instead of sleeping the day away. He yelled "Spider Man" but I said Fahrenheit 911. His face went blank as I said that I wanted him to see this movie. I could read all in his face that documentaries can't be fun, and most definitely not as good as the new Spider Man movie. I convinced him to go on the strength that I would also take him to see Spidey next time out. He was cool with that and off we went.

On the way he asked me why on his day off from school, I was sort of taking him to school? To him, documentaries meant learning something about something. He wasn't too far off with that, but I told him that this was important stuff, stuff he needed to be aware of in the many games people play with and on one another. I'm from the mean and often times confusing streets of Harlem, USA, and though we were caught-up in it, we learned early on to pickup on the bull coming from up and around any corner. But my son is a 15-year-old just starting to piece things together in recognizing that all people aren't nice, that the inviting nature of a smile and a handshake can be like a deathtrap, that promises can be outright lies and that death can be much closer than you ever think. I guess these words were a bit confusing for the kid, as what he was about to see was going to be a lot different than what he has come to know in the sanctity of a small New Jersey town, playing baseball and being on a state champion football team.

As we entered the theater there were only maybe eight people in the entire joint, and I bet Brandon that there probably wouldn't be 10 people there for the movie. After all, this town seemed a bit behind the times and most likely more republican than not. I told him, right before the movie started about 10 minutes late, that this is one of those things that make you think, that make you go, *"Hmmmmmmmm."* 15 minutes into it, with 12 people in the theater and a lost bet to pay, he looked at me and went *"Hmmmmmmmmm."* I think it was during one of the many times Moore showed our President in a compromising position, unsure of himself, of what to do or how to do it. Almost like a little kid trying to think of a lie with his face and expressions outwardly concocting the deception.

Like in his earlier work, "Bowling For Columbine," Moore had struck gold in telling another story simply and to the point, nothing high tech or high budget about it, just predominantly the truth of the matter as illustrated in his unending search and use of Socratic questioning. He was absolutely on the money with the way he let the actions of the President and his cabinet illustrate how they had ridiculously knotted-up an already very short shoestring in this our latest war effort. Moore was simplistic and easy to understand as he asked simple questions of the people in charge, questions they couldn't answer with a straight face or many times not at all. He let their actions and sometimes cartoonish deceptions color his canvas in this documentary. In the end, it showed how susceptible we all are to a good left hook, an assortment of sucker punches and creative backslaps behind the head.

I explained the bottom-line to my boy, which is always how the have-nots or the have-not-muches find themselves ass-out, or in this case of the Iraq War: asses blown off. My son watched intensely at times at situations that even he could see were based on the okey-doke, blatant injections of stupidity and outright lies and callousness. Folks bent on quickly plastering a gaping crack spreading wildly but not able to contain or repair it. Another one of those nasty tears in our foundation that eventually makes its way to the surface costing us lives, loss of great integrity and rips us apart as a nation. He had gotten the message and in about two hours he had been permanently hipped to the bull put forth by a vast assortment of idiots and smart-ass fools, many of which we vote into office to lead us. Yesssireee, I think he got the message. Mission accomplished!

We talked about it a bit on the way home and I thought a lot about him growing up and getting closer to the nonsense that could one day take his life in such an immediate way. Just when I thought I had gotten him away from the many plagues of the streets that I came from like drugs and prison, then comes this crap wrapped in a flag with crazy suckers yelling "USA, USA, USA!" I wanted him to see that behind all the pomp and circumstance, patriotism and apple pie wasn't sweet old mom, but a machine that callously stokes a fire they can't put out. In many situations, we be the logs on the fire that simply burn into ashes and blow away in the winds.

In the end "Fahrenheit 911" reached the boiling point it was meant to reach, but it didn't fire people up enough to not put George Bush back in the White House for another term. I think the better man didn't win this one, this time. John Kerry might've taken us in a different direction, hopefully a better one. But the fire isn't meant to be put out just yet, I guess. Death and destruction must continue to rape us silly before we smack into another one of those walls that break us up into small enough pieces to realize our foolishness toward beginning again. But I have to applaud Michael Moore for his fine documentary. It was a tutelage and expose of the inner workings of the inner workings. The acting was great and real, especially the part he played as a fat man asking sophisticated people simple questions about simple things and simple people. It was shown that there were no answers to be given that were worth the loss of lives involved. It's a simple truth, nothing too complicated at all. My son got the message well-enough, as did the 10 other people in the theater that day...two people more than I thought would come to an old movie house that once perhaps was something else.

Marion Boykin, a noted boxing expert and sports aficionado, is an award-winning journalist and Internet radio host. A former sports editor, writer, television and radio personality, Boykin also gives of his time coaching kids in baseball and life. He can be heard regularly on his "Sports Box" program on the Blake Radio Network/Rainbow Soul at BlakeRadio.com.

Patriotism

by Mack Williams

It was around September 12th or 13th when the flags started appearing. In front of homes. Flying in the wind on car antennas. On the sides of office buildings and trains. On ties, scarves, jackets, lapels, and even little league uniforms.

In short, virtually everywhere.

People displayed flags to symbolize their pride in our country in the wake of the tragic events of September 11th, 2001, to honor those lost on that day, and to show solidarity with the members of the armed forces who were putting their lives on the line around the world. Most would say the flags were symbols of patriotism.

As time went on, we got further away from 9/11 and slowly but surely, the flags began to lessen in visibility, that is until the administration told us—at every available opportunity—about the imminent threat posed by Saddam Hussein and Iraq's undeniably massive stockpiles of "weapons of mass destruction."

So the flags came back for all of the aforementioned reasons and then some. No attack like that of 9/11 would ever again be visited upon the United States of America, and we were going to make that perfectly clear, effective immediately. Of course, if you believe in the principles on which this country was founded, your decision to display or not display the flag need not be based on current events. You will carry these principles with you at all times, and implement them where applicable in your life whether wearing a lapel pin or not.

Because of our continued horror at the attack on our nation, we were generally inclined to believe what we were told. God forbid what would happen if these things were true and we failed to act.

We saw the virtual dog and pony show of pictures, charts and other evidence presented to the United Nations by the then Secretary of State Colin Powell. We saw Defense Secretary Donald Rumsfeld definitively state that Iraq had WMDs and that we knew where they were, in the area around Tikrit. We heard the former National Security Advisor, Condoleezza Rice, and Vice-President Dick Cheney as they worked the talk shows to emphasize the danger we faced by not dealing with Iraq immediately.

Then we saw President Bush state these things as fact in the State of the Union and other addresses to the nation and, indeed, the world. It had to be true. Surely the President of the United States would not lie to us about a matter of such consequence. Surely the leader of the free world would not lie to the world about Iraqi freedom, and Iraq's alleged ties to al-Qaida.

Of course, other presidents have lied or been party to lies during their terms. Fresh in many peoples' memories was President Clinton's "I did not have sex with that woman" statement, which some would classify as a bald-faced lie, but nonetheless one that most men could understand and would replicate if faced with a similar situation. That, however, pales in comparison to a situation where a president would fudge the facts about something that would have us on the verge of war. Certainly President Bush would never go there.

So we were basically behind Mr. Bush in his effort to lead what he described as a "coalition of the willing" to, in his words, "disarm Iraq." The fact that probably two-thirds of Iraq had been on "no-fly zone" lockdown since Gulf War I…which would certainly have limited their ability to keep and/or procure WMDs…raised few red flags in our minds. We found absolutely no need to pause when Iraq claimed to have disarmed already, when Hans Blix and the United Nations weapons inspectors claimed progress in their efforts and needed more time, nor when most of the world and the United Nations said no and the "willing coalition" could be counted on one's hands with change to spare.

We didn't find it strange that we were rushing to war against a country that said they had no weapons, yet sought some level of dialogue with another, North Korea, which claimed to have them. Could there have been any correlation between the fact that Iraq possessed oil and the fact that we were initiating conflict with them?

Very few of us, relatively speaking, even raised an eyebrow when just prior to the "drop dead date" President Bush gave for the admission of and surrender of the WMDs—with the beginning of conflict slated to follow were this not to occur—our forces received a tip and subsequently attempted to assassinate Saddam Hussein, an action signed off on by President Bush. Some might think that such a borderline-war crimes action ought to have been cause for concern at the very least, but since all was fair in love and the war on terrorism, it was all good.

Within the next few weeks both Saddam Hussein's stature and statue were toppled, and we were told that major combat operations had ended. Now, over two years and two hundred billion dollars later, Iraq remains unstable, our death toll (to say nothing of the Iraqi fatalities) is over eighteen hundred, and we are left to wonder what our mission actually was and what really got accomplished. And what, by the way, happened to Osama Bin Laden?

How did we get ourselves in such a mess? One could argue that it is, in part, due to patriotism itself—or at least the perception of what patriotism is.

After September 11th the aforementioned outward signs meant to show patriotism were evident, and we were deathly afraid to do, say, or even imply anything that could be construed to be unpatriotic. So for a long time even veiled criticism or questioning of the president and/or administration policies was branded as being unpatriotic and, possibly worse, potentially endangering the lives of our soldiers.

As a result, many of those who might have had something to say—or pointed question to ask—bit their tongues. But were we well served by their—or should I say our—silence? In light of the devastating effect of this war on us all, the answer would clearly be no. And now in light of the release, in Britain, of the Downing Street Memo, which certainly seems to suggest that the Bush administration manipulated the facts to create a climate conducive to waging war, the answer would again be no.

Given that we are faced with another three and a half years of George W. Bush, I would hope that we come to the realization that patriotism is not solely defined by the singing of "God Bless America" at the ballgame. I hope we realize that patriotism does not require silence or acquiescence in times of crisis, but in fact calls for exchange of opinions and ideas when there is question about the direction in which we are headed.

Those who imply—for their own selfish or political reasons—that dissent is unpatriotic must never have heard of the phrase "constructive criticism." Nor would it seem they had been parents, for certainly as parents they would have encountered a situation where their child has done something which, out of love, warranted correction. Based on their logic, one would think that the child's error should not even be pointed out.

During the very sporting events at which we sing "God Bless America" the teams have people and cameras there to catch any mistakes the players may be making such that they can improve their performances, not just remain stagnant. Dissent, clearly, is not only not un-American, it follows in the tradition of some of our greatest Americans who risked and in some cases gave their lives—or at least gave up a comfortable life—to fight for what they believed was right.

As such, I hope that we will take action when needed to serve as checks and balances against the right-wing policies of an administration that believes it has all of the answers, despite all of the evidence to the contrary. With another potentially troublesome three-plus years on the horizon—both internationally and domestically—raising one's voice could be the most patriotic thing an individual can do.

About the Editor

Mack Williams is a writer whose long-running Internet column, Sportin' Life, has frequently explored the relationship of the world of sports to the world at-large, and became the basis for his first book, "Sportin' Life: Essays On Sport And Life." A producer of political radio commercials for progressive causes and candidates, he lives in the blue state of New Jersey with his wife and son. He can be reached at mcwstar@aol.com.

978-0-595-36971-3
0-595-36971-5

www.ingramcontent.com/pod-product-compliance
Lightning Source LLC
Chambersburg PA
CBHW051444280526
45785CB00003B/1416